T5-CWK-729

Miracle At Monaco

Joseph A. Tucker, Jr.

SIGNATRAN

Miracle at Monaco
by Joseph A. Tucker, Jr.

Copyright ©1998 by Signatran

All rights reserved. Printed in the United States of America.
No part of this work may be reproduced or transmitted in any form or by
any means, electronic or mechanical, including photography and recording,
or by any information storage or retrieval system without the prior written
permission of Joseph A. Tucker, Jr.

Cover Photographs: Tucker Family Archives and Hulton Getty Collection

Signatran, Inc.
P.O. 944 Virginia Beach, Virginia 23451-0944
(757) 481-2358

First Edition - Volume I
Library of Congress Card Catalog Number: 98-75080
ISBN: 0-9668007-0-2

Contents

Introduction   1

Chapter 1   Rome 1949–1950   14

Chapter 2   The Promenade – 1949   24

Chapter 3   The Monaco Question – 1950   28

Chapter 4   San Carlo — Saint Charles 1950–1951   43

Chapter 5   "My Boy, The Prince of Monaco"   54

Chapter 6   "Grandpop" and Other Honors   64

Chapter 7   Friends   79

Chapter 8   The Promenade – 1954   95

Chapter 9   Mission Accomplished 1955–1956   99

Chapter 10   Busy, Busy, Busy   137

Chapter 11   Visitors – 1958   146

Chapter 12   Septuagenarian 1959–1960   157

Chapter 13   The Promenade – 1961   168

Chapter 14   Decisions 1961–1962   172

Chapter 15   Hollywood Tomorrow – 1962   189

Chapter 16   Breaking Away 1962–1966   209

Chapter 17   The Final Years 1964–1972   220

Bibliography   233

Miracle at Monaco

Dedication

This book is dedicated to
Mary Hickey Tucker,
who fired the zeal that burned
always in
Uncle Francis.

Acknowledgments

The writing of this set of two books would not have been possible if the author's father, Joseph A. Tucker, had not collected and retained the correspondence, newspaper clippings, photographs, and personal accounts that made possible the writing about the life of his brother, Father Francis, from a family perspective. He also obtained the collection of letters, photos, and memorabilia that his mother's sister, Katie Featherstone, had saved over her lifetime. Her collections made possible the writing of the second volume, *God Was Not A Stranger.*

In 1998, the author has completed a task that he first began in 1984. He expresses his gratitude to the following for providing content and observations that have been included in the text.

The late Father Edmond B. Stout, Oblates of Saint Frances de Sales, for providing archival information about Father Tucker's stay in Monaco.

My sister, Mrs. Betty Tucker Taylor, for anecdotal material about her visits with Father Tucker in Monaco, Trieste, and Rome.

My first cousin, William Henry Tucker, for his account of his trip to Europe in 1937 with Father Tucker and other reflections.

The only other sources of substantive content are from authors who are given full identification in the text. Sources of background information about the Principality of Monaco are listed in the Appendix to *Miracle at Monaco.*

My handwriting has bedeviled the most accomplished of word processors, to whom I am ever grateful: Kathy Cebrowski, Margo Else, Claudette Johnson, Cynthia Murray, and Edith Warring.

A special thank you to Colin Finlay of the Hulton Getty Collection for permission to use of some of their photographs.

The real push and direction to complete this project has come from Liz Witkowski, proprietor of New Century Publishers, Inc., who has guided the author through the selfpublishing process. Through Liz, the author met Bill Reid, who has been masterful in editing both volumes.

Joseph A. Tucker, Jr.

Miracle at Monaco

Introduction

A dug-out
France
November 5, 1918

My Dear Joe:
    The Colonel just said to me "Father, you were brought fast
into the worst of it" — Such has been my luck, Joe — and it is
luck in one sense if I get out of it. But that's just how I feel:
"if." This afternoon I spent one very unpleasant half hour
under heavy and close fire. And last night, it was gas and
air bombs ...
    JFT

❖❖❖

8 Avenue S. Charles
Monte Carlo
March 5, 1951

Dear Joe:
    My appointment was the unexpected, unsolicited outcome
of a short acquaintance with the Monaco Family whose
members all seemed to get the impression that I was the
nearest thing to their dream-priest they ever saw. It's not really
flattering in the light of comparison with the men-of-God
they've got over here, and it's because I refused to "go their
way" that the French, once again in my short career, tried to
get rid of me, and so the young Prince (28) stepped in and set
them all on their ass by sitting my ass on the throne! So I can
tell them in all truth they can kiss my Royal Irish ass in
Snellenburg's window!

JFT

✦✦✦

Palos de Monaco
February 18, 1953

My Dear Joe:
The Consul General of France announced yesterday the French
Government has awarded me the Cross of the Legion of Honor.
It's a real distinction and in my case a victory for an
American priest in a French parish! I'm happy about it and
grateful! Love to all!
JFT

✦✦✦

To My Dear Mama
(excerpts)

... A rosy dawn
Smiled on your life
My Father dear
Took you to wife

But happy years
Were soon too fleet,
In Heaven you will
Pure joys repeat

So come to this,
My Mother be
Henceforth O Lord
Thy property.

Yet many years
To her do give:
With her in Heaven

Her sons may live. Amen.
Francis Tucker
21st June 1905

❖❖❖

March 5, 1962

Dear Joe,
To the staid royalist snobs who claim that "Princesses just
don't do what Grace is doing," my standard reply is "and
thank GOD, Grace is not doing what Princesses over here do!"
    I say she is coming back to the USA to get a breath of clean
air. And her husband wants her to.
JFT

❖❖❖

These are excerpts from letters by the very Reverend Canon John Francis Tucker written to his brother, Joseph A. Tucker, and a poem to his mother, Mary Hickey Tucker. No authentic biography has been written about this remarkable priest and he prepared no autobiography, though I encouraged him to do so.

Canon Tucker was a Family man. He dedicated his life to five families: His natural family as son, brother and uncle; his Oblate of Saint Francis de Sales family as a professed religious;

His Roman family as an in-group member of candidates to the priesthood who became Vatican careerists and one, even, a Pope;

His Italian American family, the Parishioners of Saint Anthony of Padua Parish in Wilmington, Delaware; and

The Royal Family of Monaco, as a very special person.

This book is written by a nephew who knew him as Uncle Francis. It is a family view, a perspective from the first of his five families, that natural family as son, brother and uncle. The intent is to let the man "show himself" both as a youth and young priest, and then as a seasoned veteran of the Church Militant we all belonged to before Vatican II.

Our family and other source materials suggest that the book should be in two volumes, Before Monaco and After Monaco.

The Before Monaco period is his life up to age 60. The emphasis is on his childhood, priestly formation, and early priesthood. The source materials include numerous letters written from Rome to his mother's sister, Aunt Katie, as he studied for the priesthood. The letters are presented in exerpt along with a commentary called a Family View. One can "know" Francis from them. But above all, what Mary Hickey Tucker did to ensure that her son, Francis, became a priest is the "family story" about the life of John Francis Tucker. The title of that volume is *God Was Not A Stranger*.

The After Monaco family view is based on over 80 "Dear Joe" letters written to his lifelong confidante, his oldest brother, Joseph Tucker. Often they are "let your hair down" views of Monacoan events. They reflect aspects of his personality not likely to have been shown to his other families. A zealous aging realist has supplanted the zealous young idealist. Since these letters from Monaco make frequent references to events occurring from childhood and his career prior to coming to Rome and Monaco at age 60, the author presents After Monaco as Volume I, called *Miracle At Monaco*. The basic strategy of both volumes is to take a part autobiographical, part biographical view of Uncle Francis' life.

Four or more additional biographies would be needed to fully express his participation in his other families by this man who became internationally famous as the chaplain to the Royal Family of Monaco, but was already famous nationally for his social activism as pastor of an ethnic Italian parish in Wilmington, Delaware.

A brief biographical sketch provides a setting for the "family view."

◆◆◆

John Francis Tucker was born in Wilmington, Delaware on January 8, 1889, the fourth son of Mary Hickey Tucker, whose husband, William Henry, died of typhus the previous October. Francis' brothers were Joseph, 5; Edward, 3; and William, 1.

The family was poor. Mary Tucker worked as a seamstress. All four boys began working part-time at age 5 and, except for Francis, full-time at age 12. All had an elementary education through grade 8 at Saint Peter's parochial school.

In September 1903, Francis enrolled at the Salesianum School, a new private Catholic high school staffed by the Oblates of Saint Francis de Sales, a French religious order. In 1904, he entered the Oblates as a postulant, the first American to do so. In Fall 1905, he was sent to

Rome, Italy to continue his studies for the priesthood. Brilliant as a student, he earned doctorates in philosophy and theology by age 21. He was ordained in Rome, Italy, on August 10, 1911. The young Father Tucker returned to the United States in August 1912, having spent the previous year in Biblical studies.

While in Rome, he became skilled in Italian, French, Classical Latin and Greek, and acquired a working knowledge of German and Spanish.

From 1912 until 1925, he taught at the Salesianum School except for one year overseas (1918–1919) as Chaplain with the United States Army.

In 1922, he became Provincial of the American Province of the Oblates of Saint Francis de Sales, an office he held for 16 years. It was a period of great expansion for the Oblates.

In 1924, by direct appointment from the Vatican, Father Tucker was named pastor of Saint Anthony's, a newly formed parish for the Italian community of Wilmington, Delaware. One of his achievements as pastor was to lead the Italians to considerable political leverage in the state of Delaware. He remained pastor for 25 years.

In 1949, Father Tucker was elected to become a member of the General Council of the Oblates of Saint Francis de Sales, a position that required residence in Rome.

In 1950, by a second direct Vatican appointment, he became pastor of Saint Charles, Monaco. In 1951, he accepted an invitation by Prince Rainier to serve as Chaplain to the Royal Family. In 1953, he was appointed as Canon, a member of the chapter of the Cathedral of Monaco, and was subsequently referred to as Canon Tucker.

Canon Tucker served in Monaco as pastor, chaplain, and Royal Family counselor from 1950 to 1963. His major accomplishments were his development of Saint Charles' parish and his contributions to maturation of the Royal Family of Monaco; in particular, as an important mediator in the wedding of Prince Rainier and Grace Kelly.

On Canon Tucker's return to the United States at age 73, he served as a retreat master at an Oblate facility in Wernersville, Pennsylvania for several years until ill health forced full retirement. He died in Wilmington, Delaware on November 2, 1972.

— 1 —
Rome 1949 to 1950
Gander Newfoundland

7-14-49

Dear Joe:

We were 3 hours out from here on way across ocean when they turned back — so we've lost 6 hours in the air. Some piece of mechanism, a cuff on a propeller, fell off. We got back at midnight & spent the night in the barracks. We have to wait 24 hours for the missing cuff to come from N.Y. Then let's hope! 8 priests are aboard. This may be why the bad luck occurred — I suggested they leave one off but could reach no agreement!

Thanks for coming to see me off. Tell those interested of my plight I got a good sleep & shower & shave out of the delay, & I'm in no hurry. Was so glad to see Francis & Dr. T — the old Russian son of a bitch!

Love to Edna & all
JFT

❖❖❖

JFT was on his way to Rome to begin a 12-year term as the American Province member of the General Council of the Oblates of Saint Francis de Sales after "stepping down" as pastor of Saint Anthony of Padua parish in Wilmington, Delaware.

The Francis he refers to is his namesake and nephew, John Francis Tucker, II, the third son of brother and sister-in-law,

Joe and Edna Tucker. Dr. Trumianz was the Director of the

Delaware State Hospital at which Francis was a patient suffering from schizophrenia. Dr. Trumianz was renowned as an innovative psychiatrist and for his ability to get what he wanted from the Delaware State Legislature. Father Tucker and Dr. Trumianz had disagreements in the past about application of Christian ethics to the care and treatment of mental patients. However, he was convinced that Francis would receive the best available treatment and care at this hospital, which is what happened. Francis died in 1992.

✦✦✦

At age 15, Uncle Francis was the first American to join the Oblates of Saint Francis de Sales, a Roman Catholic religious Order founded by Father Louis Brisson in France in the early 1870s. Dedicated to and guided by the charisma of Saint Francis de Sales, the Oblates are "a prayer-through-service" Order dedicated to teaching, parish work, and missionary labor. Their reach is international, with communities in Western Europe, Africa, North America, and South America.

The OSFS is organized vertically. The basic unit is a community. A group of communities is formed into a Province based on national/regional location. Each Province is led by a Provincial elected by the Province members for a 6-year term. The Provinces, in turn, are subject to a Superior General who resides in a community in Rome. He is elected for a 12-year term by the entire international OSFS membership. Subject to guidance by the Holy See, he is advised by General Counselors who are elected by and represent individual Provinces.

✦✦✦

V.J.
49 Via Dandolo, ROMA
Sept. 10, 1949

My dear Joe:
Your good and wholesome card "Gotta hand it to Ya," cheered me up a lot. Mine was a one-man fight to get what I did get; and so a real vindication by the representatives of the whole congregation who gave me a bigger vote than anyone got for any other job. There are things one cannot write but I can tell you and I will. Meanwhile be sure that I am very happy to have reached this peak to which I feel my mother's prayers got me together with my own determination to have the first American Oblate go down in history with the honor that is due her and

my family.

The fact that the boys back home are crying to have me come back is another tribute. But I won't go back; I'm here to stay and see that the Oblates are what they should be the world over. And my first job is to keep the General in his place. I'm in a position to do it and he knows it. It was from him that all the opposition to me originated and carried down to the five percenters. I've really taken on new life to do the task which I feel the old timers would want me to do to prevent the Congregation from taking a bad detour from its original purpose and spirit. I've already started to work. Don't worry. You helped me through once before. At all the shrines I have visited, I've prayed for Francis, as I do every day at mass. I'm persuaded that he is for all of us a blessing in disguise, the type of victim that stays the hand of God against the rest of us.

The Holy Father was wonderful to me; so was Cardinal Fumasoni; so are they all. They're glad to have me here, which explains why Dominick isn't. The poor guy is dumb, and you know Our Lord complained of this quality in some of his disciples, especially Peter. It's God's way of keeping us humble, and without that virtue we're but a bag of wind like so many you know. My health has been good. The greatest hardship is getting a bath and toilet paper. You can get everything else here except at times the proper seat for the rectal operation, and for a patient with an ass like mine, that is a hard shit. Wouldn't it be awful if we couldn't laugh!

Be good and take care of the old man, for that's what you are and that's what I'm getting to be. Love to all!

Remember me to Frank Grady and tell him to get ready for confession. And kiss all the old ladies for me, starting with Grandmom!

As ever,
JFT

❖❖❖

Rome 1949 to 1950
Family Views
A Few Facts

Dominick – The Very Reverend Dominick Balducelli, the Superior General of the Oblates of Saint Francis de Sales.

Jubilee – the 25th anniversary of the founding of Saint Anthony of Padua parish.

Ed – the second son of Mary Hickey Tucker, a man who had a long and losing encounter with John Barleycorn but who finished strong, Christian-wise.

Politics – religious style. Soft words – tough stances. "Hard ball" all the way. A diversion that helps make community life bearable. That's politics, religious style. JFT had a life full of it. He lost some, won most. He understood the political process and used it well.

His letter reflects his campaign to be elected to the OSFS Superior Council and his reason to want that position. But the Superior General holds the high cards. The three solemn vows upon which life in a religious order is based are Poverty, Chastity and Obedience. The latter is often by far the most difficult in practice. In theory, it means freely subjecting one's own will to the will of God. But in practice, as scoped by the rules of the Order, one's superior spoke for the "will of God." It is of extreme difficulty for men and women to acquiesce when a superior resorts to control by affirming that his or her will is the will of God. But not to accept is to be guilty of false pride, the deadliest of the seven Capital Sins.

Father Tucker had been on both sides of the "will of God" issue, having served 3 terms as the American Provincial. He knew that the integrity of the Rule and the vows must be maintained; consequently, effective diplomatic and political action must be skillfully taken. Subsequent letters will show him to have been most masterful in action.

Dominick and Francis seemed not to have liked each other, though their relationship subsequently improved. This put them in good company. The Apostles, Peter and Paul, couldn't stand each other, biblical tradition (gossip) implies, and the great Doctors of the Church, Saints Augustine and Jerome, could not be in the same room together without manifest hostility. What about brotherly love!

❖❖❖

The writer's garbled memory of a brilliant young priest's homily on love pointed out that the English word "love" has three meanings in the ancient Greek in which the Scriptures, particularly the New Testament, were written.

The first meaning, love of mankind, was raised over 200 times. This included love of God, the salvation of the human soul, the love of neighbors as thyself. Driven by love of God and his creation, one must "save his own soul" and help his neighbor save his. Dominic and Francis had no problem with this. It's what their lives were about.

The second meaning, human love, mentioned over 40 times, refers to human interactions in community, family and other social settings. It could be warm, emotional. Many Christian themes, including the Parables, direct how to use this natural human love to achieve the higher order love.

Dominick and Francis may have disagreements about "means to an end" in this regard, but not to the objective. Father Tucker's vision brought him into more than a few differences with clerics and politicians, particularly as to strategy and tactics.

The third word for love used in the Bible, used possibly no more than 6 or 7 times, meant sex. This had two connotations: the first, carnal sex — a most powerful attraction and for some, addiction. Frankly, the church has never quite figured out what to do about carnal sex (nor has anyone else). The Catholic Religious Orders have tried to banish it, punish it,suppress it, ignore it, sublimate it, preach and practice the virtue of celibacy, and give sex a very bad press.

The writer's impression of his Uncle Francis' handling of this "demon" was to take a transcendental, Olympian view by which he could, in effect, look down on but not be touched by it — a sophisticated form of sublimation. He considered himself to be "a natural celibate." When he did refer to it, it was with humor. He laughed at it — on occasion regretfully, I do not doubt. He was a virile man.

The second connotative meaning of sex is natural attraction or its absence. Individuals are attracted to each other, one on one. Man to man; woman to woman; man to woman; woman to man. "Carnal" plays but a small part, if any, in this human loving, even sensual relationship. It lacks the exploitiveness of carnal sex. Such attractions can be long lasting. They are very much present in all forms of community life. There are also, evidently, "natural" repulsions. Who can say why?

As the ditty goes: "For reasons that I cannot tell, I do not like you, Dr. Phell." Dominick and Francis did not get along.

◆◆◆

Dec. 7th 1949
11:50 A.M.
French Line
S.S. ILE DE FRANCE

Dear Joe:
... I sent to your address my Xmas greetings to all the Klan. So you don't have to carry out my first thought of getting something for them from me. I made Francis' check out to Edna.

So, cheerio! and thanks for coming to the pier even though I evaded you!

Love to all,
JFT

◆◆◆

JFT's letters often mention a "homesickness" that nagged him his entire 13-year stay in Europe. Except for his year's service as an army chaplain (1918–1919), he was home in and around family and friends in Wilmington, Delaware from 1912 to 1949. And a sizable family it had become with 40 or more nephews, nieces, grandnephews, and grandnieces who knew him as Uncle Francis, a recognition he cherished. To brothers Joe, Ed, and Bill he was Father Francis.

The Christmas greetings mentioned in this letter refer to money to be used for gifts for nieces and nephews. If time allowed, he preferred to purchase gifts himself. In their childhood years, in the 1920s and 1930s, his nieces and nephews knew Uncle Francis was Santa's helper. Gifts for everyone.

Uncle Francis was the guest of honor at every Christmas dinner, which was often delayed until he could arrive. He would eat sparingly, for his Christmas day required his making a number of dinner calls to parishioners and friends. But, for him, a visit to Joe and Edna was a joy even for an hour. His gifts to them always included a large box of fruit, cheeses, and meats from Horisks, Wilmington's finest grocer. What to give him? Always a problem.Black socks and gloves! Maybe a scarf. Edna was always concerned about that. Who was taking care of him, anyway?

✦✦✦

Institutum Oblatorum
Sancti Francisci Salesii, (O.S.F.S.)

Via Dandolo 49
Roma
Tel. 582-389
Jan. 3, 1950

My dear Joe:
... Your greetings for Xmas came on Xmas eve. They topped the celebration for me, and I am most grateful to you for them and those.

... Over here, they simply close up for practically two weeks. Around the Vatican, you can't get anything but the Pope's blessing, and you have to take a chance on getting even that. I assisted at the Pope's Xmas reception to the Cardinals, and later to the Diplomatic Corps. Very few get in at these two extraordinary functions. And then I had a place in the tribuna reserved for Knights and Chamberlains and their ladies for the opening of the Holy Door; it was most impressive. I've been kindly welcomed by Cardinal Fusamoni, by the Vatican officials of the Secretariat of State, by the men in charge of the Roman Diocesan offices, by the American College and Embassy both of the Quirinal and of the Vatican. Then pilgrims are pouring in and I have to help them and naturally do. It's good that I am busy, otherwise I'd be like a mother who had lost her only child. Each day it costs a little more to be away from home, but I experience a happiness here that can come only from the consciousness of having done the right thing in

*the right way and of still doing it. Perhaps it's true that life
begins at 60, as you say. At that age, it's high time that at least
a change of life should occur; ask Edna if she doesn't agree. ...*

*I pray for Francis everywhere and always. He is still the
greatest blessing the family has and will be higher up than any
of us in heaven.*

My love to all,
JFT

◆◆◆

It is unprecedented for a parish priest from anywhere to get the reception that Father Tucker received at the Vatican and at the Quirinal,
the Seat of the government of Italy. It is more unusual yet for an un-
titled priest to have diplomatic status with the Vatican Secretariat of
State. But it was his choice to have remained a parish priest. Family
lore has it that in the mid-1930's he was offered a bishopric (of Tren-
ton, N.J., I believe) but declined. If he had accepted, he would have
been in line for the progression to Archbishop and Cardinal. However,
if he had accepted, he would have had little opportunity to continue the
growth of the Oblates of Saint Francis de Sales and continue his career
as preacher and retreat master. Though both pastor and provincial, he
never thought of himself as an administrator.

◆◆◆

Institutum Oblatorum
Sancti Francisci Salesii

Via Dandolo 49
Roma
Tel. 582-389

January 1950
Dear Joe:
*Your wonderful, plentiful, bountiful Xmas box reached me
yesterday. ...*

Everything got here, best of all, the salted nuts which I haven't seen since I left the U.S., and the guinea, and the hot dogs, and the bacon, and butter, and bean-soup with cherry wine, and a beauty of a box of Millard's candies, and cake and — I can't count them all, but they are all here, right in my room, in the night table out of which I moved the piss-pot for the present emergency! I can't use the dear old vase anyhow in my present condition, which I explained at length to Edna. The harness to which I am hitched calls for the type of receptacle used in hospitals, or in its absence a milk bottle, because this patented invention of Dr. Bartolozzi involves some sort of geometrical ratio limiting one's gyrations to an arc of not more than 16 millimeters, which the aperture of the ordinary milk bottle assures.

Don't think that I am worried about this, although some-what annoyed. I remember Mother telling us that Grandpop Hickey was marked with a bulge that came to him from ringing Saint Peter's bell when Dewey won the battle of Manila. He died at 82, not from the hernia but, as I recall, in a fit of rage at Grandma Hickey, his second wife, for leaving lumps in his mashed potatoes. He could stand lumps in his own flesh, but not in his potatoes. Then five days later, in the blizzard of 1898, she died through sheer remorse of conscience, although Father Lyons had absolved her. I was in the death chamber when she breathed her last, and that night Ed, Bill, and I went to sleep at Mulven's while you, I believe, stayed at 603 W. 7th to help Mr. Kilroy put the ice in the bier, which might explain your later achievements as a bartender at home. I enjoy having the leisure to recall these bits of family history which should be handed down to future generations.

Love to all,
JFT

◆◆◆

The family has no record of the hernia being corrected surgically, possibly because our dear uncle seems to have acquired a certain affection for it as a nature-given hair shirt.

And now for Grandpop Hickey! Grandpop was a major influence in the early lives of his four grandsons via daughter, Mary Hickey Tucker. He helped support them after the premature death of their father in 1888. As the hickory stick yielding, demanding, dedicated school master of Saint Peter's parochial school, he was their teacher and mentor. From him, they also learned the meaning of fear of God. Many of Grandpop's former students wore lumps on their craniums as badges of honor delivered by the Hickey shillelagh. But Grandpop Hickey cannot be dismissed this lightly. He was a major factor in the growth of private, parochial education on the East Coast during the 19th century. He was not a typical Irish immigrant in that he came to the United States as a highly educated man.

Edward Butler Hickey – "Grandpa Hickey"

— 2 —
The Promenade - 1949

"Only a miracle can save us" was the Monagasque lament in the Spring of 1949. "Monsieur, I assure you we are doomed!"

"Sad, very sad! Our Prince Louis is dying and his grandson, Prince Rainier, is taking over. We are sad for both reasons."

An American tourist and a native Monagasque shopkeeper were chatting casually on a sunny April afternoon in La Condamine's beautiful terrace overlooking Monaco's harbor. The shopkeeper's concern was shared by all 3,000 native Monagasques, because their cherished status as citizens of the Principality was in jeopardy. Citizenship is one thing that cannot be bought in Monaco. It was said that, to even qualify, a family must have had permanent residency for four generations. So among the 23,000 permanent residents of the earth's most densely populated country, the native Monagasques are both respected and envied. After 800 years with the Grimaldis, they feel like relatives of the royal Family, and that brings with it the inalienable right to criticize.

"France has us now, Monsieur; France has us for sure."

"Why? And so what?," asked the puzzled tourist.

"Monaco is a family affair. We sink or swim with the Grimaldis, and this Grimaldi will sink us. Under the French we will have to pay income taxes, serve in the military, and be hassled by the French bureaucracy. But worst of all, we will have to be French!"

"I see," the tourist said as he pondered the fate of being French.

"But the Prince! What's the problem with the Prince?"

"He will kill himself or never marry. The Treaty will be broken either way. Right now at the casino 1 will get you 5 that the Treaty will be broken within 15 years."

"What treaty?"

"Our 1918 Treaty with France. We understand it to say that if a ruler of Monaco, man or woman, should die without an heir, the Principality becomes a French protectorate."

"Now I see why you are so worried. Everything is up to the Prince," said the tourist.

"Indeed, sir, indeed! And our beloved Prince loves racing cars and racy women. He is a master of curves, but the French have the roads and the women that will do him in. Then France will have what's left of Monaco."

"1 to 5 is looking good," the tourist mused — then — "What do you mean, 'What's left of Monaco'?"

"Our history is in two eras — B.C., before the Casino, and A.C., after the Casino. Little more than 100 years ago, our territory stretched east to the Italian border, but in 1848 the agriculture areas of Menton and Roquebrune declared themselves free towns. Only Monaco stayed with the new Prince — 30-year-old Prince Charles. He had lost four-fifths of his territory and his source of income. He was almost bankrupt."

"So something new was needed, a casino perhaps," the tourist interjected.

"Precisely, but not at first. The Prince wanted to develop Monaco as a health and vacation resort for wealthy continentals. That had some success, but this place was almost inaccessible except by sea. So in 1855, efforts were made to operate a casino. That floundered until 1861, when Francoise Blanc moved to Monaco and set up Le Societe De Bains Mer et Cercle des Etrangers. A most successful enterprise, my friend."

"So modern Monaco began," the tourist said.

"You must read about it, but let me show you what the shady Mr. Blanc made happen. That whole area over there where the casino is, Monte Carlo, was almost barren grazing field with sheep and a few shepherds — not much else. Where we are now, La Condamine, that means `The Field of our Lord,' was a beautiful area of flower gardens and citrus groves. Now it is our commercial center, though many of us originals still live here.

"The Rock doesn't look as if it has changed much. That is Old Monaco. What is new there since 1860 is the Cathedral and the Oceanographic Museum — and the Prince's racing cars."

"We are back to the prince again," the tourist said. "I might just look for some of that 1 to 5 money. He might fool you. He has a lot to work with here."

"Work, the magic word," the Monagasque replied. But we have not had working Grimaldis, the way you mean. They are seldom here more than four months in a year. Others do their work and the Society runs itself. That cannot be, now. Times have changed on the Riviera. Nice and Cannes have casinos. They have better beaches and easier access. Competition is building. The casino no longer carries the Principality. We need a leader, but do we have it?"

"You will soon find out, I suspect."

"Besides the Casino, we have our shops, our small businesses that manufacture liqueurs and perfumes, and a tobacco monopoly. If the French take over, they will bury us one way or another. Either they will downplay Monaco's importance on the Riviera or simply overwhelm us with new capital, new people, and new leaders."

"Please forgive me for saying so, my friend, but you Monagasques seem to need the Prince more than he needs you. He must have the wealth to take his cars and his girl friend and leave. You are demanding much from him. He must be Prince, chief executive officer, diplomat, finance officer, and a prolific father to save you."

"Your Yankee frankness is painful. Yes, he could leave, but he won't. The Grimaldis will never abandon Monaco. We have 800 years of history that says they will not. And, every one of them was in trouble one way or another. Well then, what is he going to do? We would like to know that, but I can tell you that if the tourists do not come, Monaco is no more. The casino, beach, shops, climate are not our major asset. Nice, Cannes, San Remo have those and more. What they do not have is a Prince. The Royal Family is our greatest asset. Does our young Prince realize it? We are not sure."

After a pause the shopkeeper continued, "You do not have the whole story yet. You can find the rest of it up there. Let's walk up. I'll tell you about Old Monaco on the way."

"In 1949, the commune of Old Monaco, population 1900, formed with la Condamine and Monte Carlo the independent principality of Monaco. The Rock, as it is called, is the original Monaco, functioning as a Renaissance enclave with ties to both past and present. A Genoese and Renaissance palace and a Romanesque-Byzantine cathedral provide an aura of timelessness and order. Camera-carrying tourists come here hoping for a glance at nobility. Here one thinks of Prince and Princess, of power, wealth, and religion. This seat of power is no secular business headquarters. Here, away from the shops, beaches, hotels, and casino, one realizes a fact that is so obvious that its significance is ignored. Monaco is a Roman Catholic country with centuries' old ties to the Vatican. The Prince is responsible for the spiritual as well as the temporal welfare of his subjects."

"That seems an unlikely role for Rainier III. Are the Grimaldis really serious about religion?," the tourist asked.

"Very much so in a formal way. In private, who can say? Remember the ties to Rome are ancient ones. If those ties are broken, the Grimaldis will fall soon after. We are sure the Vatican does not want that, but the clergy here are French and we doubt if they care. They are certain they will stay no matter what happens."

"That should make for a cool relationship, shouldn't it?"

"Formal and sterile describes it better. The rumor is that Prince Rainier may want more from the clergy than we are getting now."

"My God! Another problem," the tourist thought. "The odds are getting longer. And what do the French clergy do for you?," he asked.

"They baptize us, marry us, and bury us. And on special occasions, as is their custom, our holy shepherds fleece us."

"And that is it?"

"That's it. With the approval of our old and cold bishop who presides over our not-so-old-but-cold cathedral."

The American tourist bid goodbye to his friendly acquaintance with the hope that they would meet again. "A hot prince and a cold church," the tourist thought. "Trouble is brewing in River City." He headed for the casino for a drink and a bet. "Surely there must be some 10 to 1 money around. France holds very good cards."

— 3 —
The Monaco Question – 1950

Prince Rainier III of Monaco, a young man with bright ideas? Indeed, yes.

Put the railroad underground — all 2 miles of it. Use the excavated rock to capture new land from the sea.

Use the new land for beaches, roads, and light industry. Attract clean, light industry.

Have Monaco be the European headquarters for non-European companies.

Rainier wanted to modernize Monaco — make it an international center for recreation and culture. Monaco, he knew, needed an awakening. It had changed little since before World War I. The rebuilding of Europe after that war, the long worldwide depression, the 6 years of World War II, and the few years of social adjustment that followed had led Prince Louis, Rainier's grandfather, to be cautious and conservative. Monaco rode out 35 years of turbulent times successfully, but Monaco looked old, felt old, and thought old.

Prince Rainier dealt with old thinking first. When he found his ideas being tossed aside as unnecessary by cabinet members appointed by his grandfather, he started making changes. That had an awakening effect. The "Old Guard" found they now had a full-time chief executive intent upon managing, not just delegating. He would proceed with them or without.

To attract a broad base of tourists, the climate, beach, hospitality, and, above all, the Monagasque mystique must be featured. Initially the casino would be played down. That attraction would take care of itself. New tourist facilities would be needed, especially lodgings. A mini building boom was in the offing.

The native Monagasques and thousands of permanent foreign residents had to envision a new Monaco. All must pitch in and all must share. Rainier began with the sharing. Quality of life, not just money, was the issue. Liking one another, working together, sharing culturally, and having some good, clean fun — great — but how to get it started? The Prince had to keep his distance; the Royal Family mystique alone required it.

The church should lead the way, Rainier knew. In a Roman Catholic country, what he wanted had to be a spiritual awakening. That was a job for the Church. What did Monaco have? An aging, complacent, out-of-this-world, mostly French clergy, whose only concern for their parishioners was seemingly "will they be in the state of grace at the moment of death?" Blessings given, alms taken, with prayers for one and all. Complacency sanctified as tradition.

Prince Rainier knew that what he wanted would be unprecedented in Western Europe, particularly in France. He wanted a young, dynamic clergy of international composition that could spark a spiritual change in a people grown used to being considered "worldly" and who could meaningfully serve the thousands of tourists he hoped to attract to Monaco.

In 1866, the church in Monaco was separated from the Diocese of Nice as an "abby nullius" immediately subject to the Holy See. In 1887, Pope Leo XIII's *Bull Quemodmodum* created the Diocese of Monaco. Quemodmodum was an agreement between the Pope and the Prince of Monaco that, in 1949, still regulated the juridical condition of the church in Monaco. According to the agreement, the government defrays the expenses of religion and enjoys extensive privilege including that of presenting a trio of names for episcopal appointments, nomination of all pastors except that of Saint Charles in Monte Carlo which is reserved permanently to the religious order, the Clerks Regular of Mother of God.

In 1950, the Diocese of Monaco had 5 parishes, 15 diocesan and 20 religious priests, 60 brothers in 5 communities, 130 nuns in 7 convents, and 2900 students in 10 Catholic schools. Monaco enjoyed diplomatic relations with the Holy See and maintained a minister plenipotentiary in Rome. Following the agreement with the Vatican, the principality erected in Old Monaco the Cathedral of the Immaculate Conception.

In Prince Rainier's view, the parish of Saint Charles in Monte Carlo was the preferred one for the change he envisioned. The congregation was made up largely of working class people, most of whom were either French or Italian citizens. Only a minority were aristocrats. Since it was in Monte Carlo, many tourists were drawn to it. If change was possible, Saint Charles was the place to begin. Unfortunately, Saint Charles was the parish over which he had the least influence.

In spite of the diplomatic risks, the Prince decided to take his problem directly to Pope Pius XII. A proper presentation was critical. He had to avoid the impression that his request was based on a personality conflict with the clergy at Saint Charles, a desire to secularize religion, to alter the agreement with the Vatican, or to assume the prerogatives of the French Bishop of Monaco. The Pope would have to be assured that Rainier's concern was for the spiritual welfare of an increasing international Catholic Community.

Early in 1950, Pius XII granted the Prince of Monaco a private audience to discuss matters of state. The Prince left reassured. The Pontiff had received his request kindly and indicated that the Vatican would give it prompt consideration.

◆◆◆

Monsignor Domenico Tardini, the Vatican Pro-Secretary of State and a skilled diplomat, was assigned the "Monaco Question."

Monsignor Tardini, a Roman, had a long career as a professor and Vatican official. A brief biography describes him as "upright and loyal, somewhat rough externally, thorough and exact in comprehending and solving problems — an outstanding statesman. His mind and glance were penetrating. A statesman much interested in social problems." Appointed a Cardinal in 1958, as Secretary of State for John XXIII, he helped write Mater et Magistra, the arrangements for the historic conference, Vatican II, though his own views were more conservative than those of the Pope. He died in Rome in 1961.

Monsignor Tardini did not underestimate the diplomatic implications of the Prince's request. He had several tasks to accomplish before he could assure Pius XII that the Prince's request could be met. A request that the Pope hoped to support.

Was it diplomatically feasible? Though the Italian and French governments might take a "wait and see" position, the clergy, particularly the French, were likely to be alarmed. Quemodmodum should be maintained. The Vatican must not appear to "knuckle under" to the young Prince. The Prince, too, would need to be protected from criticism for breaking national tradition. A new mission at Saint Charles would have to be successful. Could a religious order and a religious leader be found to take over at Saint Charles and perform under relentless publicity and inevitable opposition? Monsignor Tardini's aide exclaimed "all the

Prince wants is a parish priest who is a diplomat, politician, linguist, psychologist, reformer and yet young, active, vital, and not afraid of the job."

"Is that all?," said Tardini. "I know just the man and he is only sixty-one."

❖❖❖

"Francis, what do you make of it?," Domenico Tardini asked.

"The Holy Spirit must be our guide, but we can do it, Monsignor."

Archbishop Tardini had informed Father Tucker of the Prince of Monaco's request, of Pope Pius XII's reaction, and the diplomatic nuances. Would Father Tucker study the situation in preparation for a further discussion of it in a few days?

In his study, Father Tucker detected in the young prince an equalitarian bent and a political sophistication that few suspected. He liked what he perceived. This young man had the potential to give new meaning to the word Prince in the 20th century. His approach to Pius XII was forthright; the odds were that he was prepared to live with the consequences of a dramatic change at Saint Charles parish.

The removal of the Clerks Regular of the Mother of God from Saint Charles would be unfortunate but justified. They were a small Italian order with fewer than 100 priests and no international composition or experience. That they could not meet Monte Carlo's need for an international religious order was clear. It was also clear that Father Tucker's own Oblates of Saint Francis de Sales added up to a religious order that could be assigned to the parish of Saint Charles. Father Tucker was one of them — a providential package.

Founded in the early 1870's in Annecy, France, about 100 miles above Monaco, by a Father Brisson, the Oblates had a religious rule based largely on the writings of Saint Francis de Sales, a sixteenth century Bishop of Savoy in Southern France. His social philosophy has had a profound influence on the modern church.

The Oblates of Saint Francis de Sales were French.

They were also international. They had provinces in most of western Europe, including France, Italy, Germany, Austria, and the Netherlands; also two provinces in the United States, and in South America and Africa.

❖❖❖

"What do you think he is really asking for, Francis?," Tardini continued.

"He is asking for our help in preserving and changing the principality. Saint Charles is his vehicle for getting that help."

"That is the Vatican's perception also. A remarkable young man, but he will need spiritual direction of the most astute kinds."

"And, Monsignor, there must be a Princess."

"My friend, Francis, that will be your greatest challenge."

In that manner, the Pro-Secretary of State informed Father Tucker that he was the Holy Father's choice to resolve the Monaco Question.

The two agreed that much diplomatic work was required before complete assurance could be given to Pius XII. The Vatican agreed in principle that the Oblates of Saint Francis de Sales be assigned to Saint Charles, but the reaction of the Grimaldis to the Vatican's proposal would have to be determined. A month of diplomatic activity began. An informal meeting was arranged for Father Tucker to meet the Royal Family. The Grimaldis were thrilled by the Vatican's interest. They were incredulous that a Father Tucker really existed. The Royal Family's cooperation made it possible for the Vatican to act quickly. On Holy Thursday, April 1950, Monsignor Tardini handed Father Tucker a Papal document assigning to the Oblates of Saint Francis de Sales the parish of Saint Charles in Monte Carlo.

Dear Joe received three letters in 1950 about his brother JFT's move to Monaco that supported the "factual conjecture" that has just been presented.

April 13, 1950

Dear Joe:
A long time ago, I rec'd a letter from Edna saying a letter from you was to follow with news of the parish. I kept waiting from day to day, hoping, asking myself should I write and let our

letters cross or what. Well, no word from you has reached these parts so far, so I give up waiting and want to let you in on some news of mine before you get it by the grapevine.

For the last month, I have been transacting important matters at the Vatican dealing with the Principality of Monaco with the result that on Holy Thursday the Secretary of State handed me a Papal Document assigning to the Oblates the Parish of San Carlo in Monte Carlo, Monaco. The assignment calls for my going there as Pastor without giving up the charge of Councilor General of the Oblates. It is to be revamped, reorganized and put on an international basis by request of the Prince of Monaco. Three other Oblate priests and two brothers are to go with me. It's the biggest thing that has ever yet happened to the Oblates anywhere.

Strange, it's the second time the Holy See itself has assigned to me a pastorate. I'm glad to get it, both for the recognition and for the change from the Oblate community in Rome, which is the most unbearable one in the worldwide outfit. I love Rome and might add that Rome has started to love me. I have here a list of friends running up like the one at home, among great and small.

With God's help, I'll get a few in Monte Carlo too.

What will the boys say when the news gets out? Tuck and his big time Bingo! The cold facts are, I got this assignment for the Oblates. I am most happy to do something for them in Europe where they were dying. Of course, all sorts of rumors will float the air, but two things remain solid: the Secretary of State suggested my name to the Holy Father, treated the whole matter with me personally, and insisted that I retain residence in Rome as member of the Council. I'll have to live in Monte Carlo, but I'll commute to report to the Vatican, which holds direct jurisdiction over the Principality. I don't want you to publish any of this, though you are free to say you heard something about my going on an errand for the Pope. I want you to know the lowdown and the facts in the case. Tell Ed about it and Helen if you can. I'm very busy and will be more and more.

Do drop me a line, not a whole book, just a line. And give my love to all. I was in all this business when your birthday popped around and could only pray that you'd live eighty more.

Say an extra one for me. Monte Carlo has broken many a man!

With every best blessing,
JFT

♦♦♦

The Raskobs preceded the Kennedys as America's wealthiest Catholic Family. John Raskob, a financier associated with the Du Ponts and later on his own, was financial backer for Al Smith's presidential bid in 1928. Later he established the Raskob Foundation, a non-profit philanthropic organization that provides "seed money" support for religious-based projects worldwide.

♦♦♦

V + J
8 Avenue S. Charles
Monte Carlo, Monaco
Joseph A. Tucker

Dear Joe:
At last I can give you my "home-address" — the above, a rectory, if you please even tho' I had to wait 25 years to get one, and it is a beauty of a building belonging to the Prince, overlooking the sea, connected with the Church by a cloister, rooms spacious and high. The only draw-back for the present, the good Fathers who were ordered by the Pope to give up the parish to the Oblates took every bit of furniture with them including the bathtub, which they yanked out with its moorings. All this in humble protest against the August decision of the Pontiff! So we 3, Fathers Shugrue, Pennel, and I, started on 23 May with 3 straw mattresses, a chair apiece. We went out and

bought toilet utensils and enough plates and dishes to feed from, and happily came upon an excellent cook, a fine good woman who knew how to provide from the beginning.

This has been a difficult mission to be sent on and everybody, from the Vatican officials down to the French Consul and Bishop and Government officials of Monaco, are agreed that it was handled well, for which I thank God. I've carried my Mother's picture all along the route, so that the dear Lady has travelled some by air, and land and sea. I feel that she has helped me.

The enclosed clipping written by a British reporter, Anglican of course, will tell you about the local reaction. It's been an ordeal for me, left on my own in every way, financially, politically, and religiously, to work out the crazy puzzle! And this since March 6th. From April 26 to May 25, I was on the road most of the time between Monte Carlo, Rome, Paris treating with Pope and Prince and Superiors and Politicos and all involved in a most unusual church-state deal. Of course, I've missed some pilgrims in Rome, but personally I don't regret it, they were running me ragged. I shall go to Rome off and on, but my headquarters are here for a while, and I hope for a long while, it's really a break after being under at Via Dandolo for 8 months!

Let me hear from you. Tell Ed Tucker of my change. They need a couple of American bartenders at the Casino? Give my love to all the family and its branches — Hazel and hers, and the friends who keep interested in me. Tell Edna to let me know about Francis. The 3 of you should come over here and forget the rest of the world for a time. I'd take care of you. You'd enjoying selling religious articles over here; such as are sold, are found in shops that feature dirty post cards alongside the Holy ones! I'm getting cross-eyed picking out the holy cards!

Love to all!
JFT

❖❖❖

A rocky start! It would have been even more notable if the good fathers had stolen the "john" also. Accounts have it that when Father Tucker deplaned at Nice airport, his few graying locks covered by a crumbling black fedora and wearing a black business suit and clerical collar, he heard a lady in the waiting reception group explain, "Mon Dieu, a Protestant." Then as he walked to an awaiting Simca, a sympathetic woman said to him, "Poor Father Tucker! You'd have an easier time as a missionary to the Hottentots than you will have here" (he "found out she was right," he observed later).

Father Tucker kept to himself his hope that he would remain in Monaco a long while. Actually, during his 13 years there, he never let it seem to "the powers that be" that he personally wanted anything, a strategy that kept him free, independent, and often broke.

◆◆◆

Father Tucker began by letting it be known to both Prince and parishioners that he considered his initial assignment as pastor a temporary one, possibly no more than six months. He hoped to set a course for a successor. This strategy removed pressure from the Prince to choose a new chaplain for the Royal Family and allowed for a change in tactics if his own should fail. Then, his assistants and he proceeded to follow established routine at Saint Charles while they observed its effects.

◆◆◆

"George, what was your reaction to offering our operatic-style High Mass?," Father Tucker asked.

"I felt that I could have walked from the sanctuary and no one would have known I was gone," Father Shugrue replied.

"As for me, I felt as I gave the sermon that few were listening. No doubt that has happened but never was it more obvious," Father Tucker said.

The two priests were discussing the late Sunday morning High Mass at Saint Charles. For years, this Mass had featured operatic performances by noted professionals. It had become a weekly cultural event. If one were serious about attending Mass, one went to a different Mass.

Father Tucker continued, "What do you think of our Sunday Mass schedule, George?"

"Father Francis, if our parishioners really came to Mass, we couldn't handle them. We need two more and a better schedule."

"I agree. We will announce a new schedule next Sunday," the pastor promised.

"Father Francis, I've noticed also that there are not many coming to the front of the church. Those seats reserved for the wealthy are not heavily occupied," noted Father Shugrue.

"And what are the imperious ones paying for that noble privilege?," Father Tucker inquired.

"About 200 francs a year," Father Shugrue responded.

"What! a token to keep the poor in their place. That, too, will be taken care of by next Sunday."

"There are other matters we must get to immediately. We must get the congregation more involved in the Mass and parish activities. We should introduce congregational singing, as a start," Father Tucker continued.

"I feel strongly we should consider lowering the First Communion age from 12 to 7, as it is everywhere else," added Father Shugrue.

"George, we will use revolution rather than evolution here. One could easily be seduced into inaction in this sunny place for shady people. While we are at it, we will get rid of the first, second, and third class weddings and funerals. That's just more of that social class nonsense that has no place in the Church," said Father Tucker, his classic Irish face turning red as he warmed to his subject. "We will start by giving the boot to the opera singers."

"Revolution it is," said Father Shugrue as he checked to see if he had the cab fare to the Nice airport.

The following Sunday at all Masses, Father Tucker announced the end of the opera era. "I am the Star here," he proclaimed.

Said Father Shugrue to Father Pennel, "He couldn't be more sincere."

◆◆◆

The revolution was successful, but it had repercussions. The working class people loved the changes. The number of communicants increased greatly.

However, there were critics among the upper classes and aristocracy. Many of them came around when they realized that the removal of offensive class distinction symbols had done them no harm whatsoever and had made their relationships with their Monacoan neighbors much more pleasant. But the French clergy, from Bishop Riviere to the lowliest curate, moved from shock to dismay to outright fury. The revolution was aimed right at them, and "That American" continued to pour it on. Many communicants of other parishes were attracted to Saint Charles to participate in the dynamic services and to hear the masterful sermons by Father Tucker, whose skills as an orator rivaled that of the famous Monsignor Fulton Sheen.

The clerical complaints reached the Prince and surprised him not at all. "At last, they have someone else to criticize. Thank God for Father Tucker," he thought. The Vatican's new team had his support.

Father George Shugrue, a Philadelphia-born Oblate, was to be Father Tucker's right hand man for the next several years, and was hand-picked, as this letter shows.

April 11, 1950
Reverend George Shugrue

Dear George:
On Holy Thursday, Monsignor Tardini, Secretary of State for Extraordinary Ecclesiastical Affairs, handed me a document to deliver to Father General whereby the Holy Father assigned to the Oblates the parish of San Carlo in Monte Carlo, Monaco.

Monsignor Tardini had been treating of this matter with me since March 5th. The first reaction of Father General and of Father Dufour was that "we couldn't handle it" — lack of "elements" — fear of danger to observance of the Rule, etc. UNTIL I said: "I'll go!," and then leaping with joy even as John the Baptist did, they both agreed.

I told them at that time that I would ask you to assist me to take over this parish, and they approved of this choice.

. *I have written to Father Buckley about this. Father General suggested that I await Father Buckley's answer before writing to you, but it is my better judgement to advise you at once lest any plans you might be formulating suffer one way or the other by your not knowing it.*

My reasons for wanting you:

1) You are an element! all geared for the task by your knowledge of French and German.

2) Your sociability makes you the person for the type of people one meets at Monte Carlo.

3) You can play golf with the Prince, who agitated the question of making this church and parish international and of getting another order than the one now there — Clerics of the Mother of God — to take over.

4) I'll need a chauffeur.

5) You were contemplating staying over another year anyhow, perhaps for the Sorbonne.

We shall have with us a Frenchman (perhaps Pennell), and an Italian (Canova), and 2 brothers.

Monsignor Brennan of Philadelphia and the Rota made a canonical visitation of this parish last year and recommended a clean sweep. He told me it is a gold mine, and that's all the Mother of God boys considered it, letting all priestly work go by, and even giving scandal.

While the matter of the assignments is not a secret because it has been concluded, the matter of asking for you is and should remain such till Father Buckley answers.

Write me and let me know if you are willing. Thanks for your card.

With all my love!

◆◆◆

With Father Shugrue and the other Oblates, Father Tucker began the reform of Saint Charles Parish with some of the more dramatic changes occurring in the remaining months of 1950.

The liturgical and sacramental issues effectively dealt with, Father Tucker turned next to the social life of the parish. His particular concern was the children. Changes in the social area would take much longer, he knew, and could not simply be ordered by him as pastor. So in the late Fall of 1950, he thought it time to report to Monsignor Tardini at the Vatican. He reported in detail about the changes at Saint Charles and the progress that had been made. He was frank about reporting the opposition that had arisen among the French clergy and a minority of aristocratic circles. He was, he said, prepared to return to Rome if his continuing at Monte Carlo could lead to embarrassment for the church or the prince.

Monsignor Tardini replied, *"Francis, we would like you to stay a while longer at Monte Carlo. The Prince has asked for it, and the people of Monaco have petitioned it."* On November 1, 1950 Father Tucker wrote, *"I go back on the 3rd and am very happy to go back under such auspices. It's really a lovely place there and, were it not for the dam French, it would be the best."*

Father Tucker wrote "dam." He never wrote "damn." The "dam French" were the local French clergy, especially Bishop Reviere "that cold, old frog." The "noble French" were his working class parishioners, their relatives and a growing host of admirers.

More factual conjecture!

Nov. 1, 1950

My dear Joe:
I've just come in from the most sublime ceremony I have ever attended, and the fact is I have attended a variety of them and quite a few. It's now quarter past noon, and I have just reached the house which I left this morning at 6:30 to attend the Promulgation of the Dogma of the Assumption of our Lady. One could choose to assist at the Promulgation itself in the open, in front of Saint Peter's facade, or at the Papal Mass inside, but not at both. I chose the former and am glad I did, though it meant standing 3 hours straight. People had waited all night around Saint Peter's Square, even those with tickets to get the vantage points. I had a fine place in the Loggia, that is

on the roof of Bernini's great colonnade where they had built tribunes like bleachers from which you could look down on the proceedings. 600 Bishops, the most Rome has seen since the Vatican council in 1870 — 40 Cardinals, so many priests that I was ashamed to be one; they ought to go to work! And a million people easily extending from Saint Peter's to the Tiber in a solid mass, besides the 30,000 inside the church. Beautiful weather! The whole mob singing and cheering and as silent as a Trappist when the Pope asked them to pray, in silence. I sang with the different groups in Latin, Italian, English, and French, and cheered in German and Spanish. Could not keep up with the Poles! I prayed for you all, especially Francis. I came from Monte Carlo to attend this ceremony and to assist at a General Council meeting at which things are finally going a bit more my way, since I put the OSFS on the map in Europe in the eyes of the Vatican. Monsignor Tardini, the Pope's Secretary of State, asked me to stay a while longer at Monte Carlo; he told me the Prince has asked for this and the people of Monaco had petitioned it. So cheerio! I go back the 3rd, and am very happy to go back under such auspices. It's really a lovely place there and, were it not for the dam French, it would be the best.

My love to all!

♦♦♦

Father Tucker did return to preside over what an astounded French Press called Yankee Vaudeville. This chapter ends with a touch of family whimsy.

Monte Carlo
Nov. 21, 1950

Dear Joe:
Fourteen years ago today, Mary E. Tucker, C. of M. (child of Mary), left us for a while. Bill, who always did try to get the

lead on the rest of us, advanced his meeting with her, but surely not by many years over our own rendezvous. Last evening, I spent a couple of hours reading over some letters she left me. In one, written to me at Rome (1911), she says: "Joseph, thank God, is all gold." I take it that with FDR, you went off the Gold Standard; however, it's nice to think of the days when you were a mountebank.

Perhaps Mother had told Edna of this before your marriage, which, if so, would constitute grounds for annulment under the title of substantial error. Of course, Edna would have to start the proceedings. I know a Monsignor in the Rota here at Rome who might take the case, thus permitting her to enter the Visitation Monastery and you the Trappists, under oath to never consort again. One unpleasant feature of such a scheme to procure for yourselves old-age security would be that the decision would make your children illegitimate and their children little bastards in the second degree. This inconvenience could be solved by having them all move to Monte Carlo where the majority of the population is so constituted, without any civil injunctions. Just what M.E.T. and Mother Mac in heaven would do over all this is not hard to surmise: Lucifer's rebellion would pale in significance with the battle these dear souls would stage. So I would advise Edna to consult her big Sister, Hazel, about it, and you might take the matter up with Ed, our brother, and with Helen Tucker so as to have the whole family in on it. But don't mention it to the children or Laura or the Jeandells. I hate to think of it myself and wouldn't have if I hadn't read those letters last night.

Thanks and all my love to all of you. I'm well, but as homesick as ever for all of you, especially Francis. Cheerio!
JFT

— 4 —
San Carlo & Saint Charles
1950 to 1951

Father Tucker took a surgical approach to making Saint Charles a "true parish." Most of the changes were in place by the end of 1951 and "made safe" by the installation of a new bishop at Monaco in 1953. His 25 years as founding pastor of an Italian community parish, Saint Anthony's in Wilmington, Delaware, was the experience that made him so sure-handed at Monte Carlo — that plus his assurance of the support of the Royal Family of Monaco. He tested those waters by stating that his initial assignment was temporary, only to get the Oblates installed, and then made some changes at Saint Charles that would "drain blood" from the privileged. Once assured of support by both Vatican and Royal Family, he proceeded Tucker-style — bombast, punch and counter-punch, guile, gall, and guts. Win the people and you've won the war. But, above all, perform.

The changes at Saint Charles were spiritual, liturgical and social. No special privilege for the privileged. No "Stars" (other then himself). Children to be seen, heard and catered to — American style.

The "crazy American" now had the not-totally-unwelcome attention of the French press who had been observing the goings-on at Saint Charles while wallowing in the vituperous "inside info" in the gossip capital of Europe. Prince-watching had been joined by Tucker-watching. The French press reported the Saint Charles story as melodrama — a Catholic priest who rode around Monaco on a motor scooter drumming up interest in a soccer team, signing up members for a school band, dispersing bubble gum to and buying ice cream cones for children, frolicking with the poor children at Lorvatto beach, clad in a black bathing suit, and who rarely appeared in public wearing a cassock was a sitting duck.

They lampooned him unmercifully. "Yankee Vaudeville" they proclaimed. "We prefer 'Yankee Vaudeville' to 'French Comic Opera'," the working class Monacoans responded. "La pere Tookaire" was their friend. What had the French press ever done for them?

His Serene highness, Prince Rainier, with his own prestige at risk for sponsoring the "Yankee Vaudeville," was a well-informed observer of the melodrama. The changes at Saint Charles were going his way. The parish was more international, the parishioners more involved. Though Father Tucker's "surgical approach" may have left the prince somewhat abashed, he recognized its strategic merit. Indeed, he welcomed the international press' attention to affairs in Monaco. "Long live the melodrama," he could say. No doubt he would have been even more abashed and, at times, amused by sentiments expressed in JFT's letters about his life in Monaco.

◆◆◆

February 23, 1951

Appointment of an American Priest as Royal Family Chaplain

For what is probably the first time in history, an American priest has been appointed Grand Chaplain of a reigning Royal Family of Europe. Word has been received by the Very Reverend William D. Buckley, OSFS, Provincial of the American Provincial of the Oblatesof Saint Francis de Sales, that his predecessor as Provincial, the Very Reverend J. Francis Tucker, OSFS, has been appointed Grand Chaplain of the Sovereign House of Monaco. The decree appointing Father Tucker to this post was signed by His Supreme Highness, Prince Rainier III, Ruler of the Principality of Monaco, and dated February 16th, 1951.

Father Tucker, who has been serving for the past year as Pastor of Saint Charles' Church, Monte Carlo, and who will continue that work, will have under his supervision all religious services conducted in the Royal Palace. His fluency in several languages, including French and Italian, make him peculiarly fitted for pastoral duties in an international capital such as Monte Carlo. For twenty-five years, he served as Pastor of Saint Anthony's Italian Parish in Wilmington, Delaware.

Reverend Joseph F. Niedermaier, OSFS
Secretary of the Provincial

◆◆◆

8 Avenue S. Charles
MONTE CARLO

March 5, 1951

Dear Joe:
Your good, much desired letter of Feb. 28th came today.
Thanks for the enclosure which in terms of 1,750 francs is
considerable money over here — as a matter of fact, what
one gets for 12 masses! The new Princely job pays in
prestige and honor more than in cash! As Pastor of Saint
Charles, which I remain, I draw monthly 32,000 francs
which is roughly 100 dollars. The take-in on Sundays
averages 50 to 60 dollars on the basis that the Government
pays the upkeep for church property. It's certainly NOT the
stand I used to have! — albeit I do have a beautiful HOME!
   My appointment was the unexpected, unsolicited
outcome of a short acquaintance with the Monaco Family
whose members all seemed to get the impression that I was
the nearest thing to their dream-priest they ever saw. It's
not really flattering in the light of comparison with the
men-of-God they've got over here, and it's because I refused
to "go their way" that the French, once again in my short
career, tried to get rid of me, and so the young Prince (28)
stepped in and set them all on their ass by setting my ass on
the throne! So that I can tell them in all truth they can kiss
my Royal Irish ass in Snellenburg's window! — as Joe Kelly
so often quoted.
   No! I am not coming home this year: the harness is
working O.K., and I am in no way bothered except by the
morning struggle to get my protruding guts into the dam
straps: once in, they stay put. Of course. I can't play foot-
ball! My appointment stirred not only the Principality, but
very much the Vatican and the French Government — to the
extent that I am running a close second to Stalin as the most

feared man in Europe. Naturally, I'm having a hell-of-a-good time!

 Love to all
 JFT

✦✦✦

Our beloved Uncle was not given to understatement. The throne his ass ended upon was the position of chaplain to the Royal Family of Monaco, a position that made him a member of the inner circle. Actually, Father Tucker was moved deeply by the Prince's invitation. The Prince was answering both the pastor's and his own critics with a highly visible reaffirmation of royal policy. His Serene Highness announced the appointment by official proclamation. The announcement was a bombshell. It was totally unexpected, since no American previously had been appointed to be a chaplain to a Royal Family in Europe.

Father Tucker kept the revolution going as he took on the additional responsibility of Chaplain to the Royal household. At a palace meeting at which he was introduced to the 70 or more members of the Palace staff, he announced that he wished to be Chaplain to all of them. In the past, a royal chaplain served only the royal family. And he requested that the long-unused palace chapel be made available for religious services. The Prince agreed and paid for its refurbishing himself.

"Rainier had asked him to come closer," Father Tucker knew. Gratified, he could take on that "greatest challenge," a Princess for the Prince and Principality. He knew how crucial that choice would be to assuring that the Prince's visions for Monaco would be fulfilled.

An aside! His mother, Mary, was not responsible for his assigning social roles — kicking and kissing — to the human ass. Most likely, he learned about these usages from the humorous, iconoclastic Aunt Katie who at every Christmas gathering would announce her presence grandly with "Merrie Chris-me-ass!"

16 April 1951

Dear Joe:
I don't know whether I let you know that I got your Easter contribution to the Royal bank account! Thanks! A God-send

even to one of Princely surroundings. If anything, my obligations are greater than during mere plebeian days! l am terribly busy, more so than ever in my life, if one can imagine that! This whole dam Principality is on my neck, rather a novelty for them to have a priest who's not a parasite!

The parish keeps me going, because I am making it a parish! But the Palace keeps me on a constant grind: everybody that's anybody has to meet the Chaplain, to the extent that Queen Victoria-Eugenia of Spain felt obliged to send her Lady-in-waiting to excuse her Majesty for not attending my Mass! I sent back word: "Tell the old girl to never do it again!" Tomorrow, lunch with the Consul of France; Saturday, with Vatican Ambassador and Italian Consul. Sunday, with Lolla, my cook. I am home-sick to the brim!

Love to Lady Edna; cheerio to Lord Joseph Aloysius himself!

JFT

◆◆◆

June 6, 1951

Dear Joe:
Only when I get to Rome can I take time to sit at a desk and do some writing. I'm here for the Beatification of Pius X, whom I knew for six years ('06 to '12). Quite something to see a personal acquaintance make the grade! I must come here occasionally for Oblate business too, and this time also on business for the Prince who seems to like me — possibly because I'm the first priest who has ever dared to show a truly priestly interest in him. He's a swell boy. Am sure that if Betty weren't married to Bill Taylor, or Phyllis to Cliff, or Mary to Joe, Prince Rainier would not hesitate to marry any one or all three of them!

Right now his little playmate is a pretty movie actress, Gisele Pascal! I've got a job on my hands, baby! It's queer for

*me to be moving around these Princes and their like, but I
move in such a manner that it's always their turn to move next.
I give the bastards to understand that Mary Hickey's legitimate
son is doing them honor, and not the reverse. Naturally, the
local clergy, with Bishop on top, can't take it. I've put Saint
Charles' parish on the map — it's outstanding among parishes
in France simply through a bit of American common sense,
which the people love. A contrast with the sanctimonious
inefficiency of priests holier-but-not-as-good!*

*I'm well. Homesick, aging, angry with the surroundings,
having fun just the same!*

Love to all!
JFT

◆◆◆

June 7, 1951

Dear Joe:
*I had only returned from mailing you the letter of the 6th at
Vatican City Post Office when yours of May 31 arrived, the US
francs safely tucked in and most gratefully received. Since I got
the job with the Prince, all handouts have ceased, my erstwhile
good friends thinking without doubt that it would be infra dig
for the Chaplain of the Palace to be handed some dough. It
would like hell! is all I can say to that lese-majesty scruple.
Why, I gave the Prince a pack of Chesterfields the last time I
saw him, and he thanked me profusely. On the contrary, the list
of beggars that line up on me on account of the appointment is
unending. At the head of the procession come the down-and-out
royalty who can't touch the Prince but can touch his chaplain
and do.*

*King Farouk sat on an air-cushion when here at Monte
Carlo, only he had one of his suite carry it around for him and
make a bow as he squatted his royal reredos thereon. I'm all
right on that score, but the front of my anatomy becomes more*

uncomfortable under the increasing pressure of the saddle, and I have to lie down now and then to get me breath and me ball-bearings in the socket. Happily, the cassock permits me to do the arranging even in mid-street; I pretend I'm looking for my beads, and finally triumphantly pull them out of an adjacent pocket. Cheerio!

 Love to Edna and Francis!
 JFT

✦✦✦

July 28, 1951

My Dear Joe:
I am about to leave Rome for Holland where I want to cel-ebrate the 40th anniversary of my Ordination with the Dutch Provincial, the only other remaining member of my Ordination class. I don't want to celebrate at Monte Carlo because I'm not there long enough as yet, and I've stirred them up enough without adding oil to the flame! The Princely Family is royal and loyal to me, and therein lies the rub — the local clergy! Frenchmen uber alles! The bastards won't stoop to kiss a Royal Irish ass and, after all, who can blame them! Joe Kelly must be drunk with heavenly joy at the sight! — and Mary Hickey Tucker demanding more jewels in her celestial crown! The 40th year has been the toughest and the most productive, for I brought the OSFS under International spotlight and made the first inroad into French ecclesiastical policy that the Vatican Diplomatic Service has ever known. Of course, they're tickled to death — I mean the Italians!

 I have just this morning left the Secretary of State's office after a half-hour interview with the Boss of it, my classmate Monsignor Tardini! How the old clock turns around and the pendulum swings! Things are much brighter for me among the OSFS over here since luck came my way. Nothing the General can't do for me now! It's been tough sleighing, but I mean to make the last long mile my best effort! Been tough on you folks at home too, I'm quite aware! 'Twould have been tougher if I hadn't done it!

Love to all! Edna, Francis! I need addresses of others! Cheerio!

JFT

A Perspective

The previous four letters need little embellishment. It was remarkable that Father Tucker accomplished so much in so little time (15 months). The significance of his accomplishments may be highlighted by a brief historical review of Vatican policy during the latter period of the papacy of Pius XII. Pope Pius XII, an absolutist who concentrated Church rule in the Vatican, was during his papacy locked in a struggle with Communism. From 1944 until his death in 1958, he managed the Church with two Pro-Secretaries of State (formally in 1952) and a handful of trusted associates. At the time that Father Tucker went to Rome in 1949, the Pro-Secretary of State for Ordinary Affairs was Monsignor Montini, who later became Pope Paul VI. They were acquainted, having been schoolmates but not classmates, since Montini was about 9 years younger.

Montini's responsibilities covered the broad area of religious issues. He was known as a liberal with socialist leanings who supported the role of Christian Democratic parties throughout Europe. For him, such parties were "a social action" vehicle for opposing Communism. He strongly influenced Pius XII's efforts to cope with a rapidly changing world, but when the worker priest movement in France became controversial and the Italian Christian Democrats lost control of parliament in 1953, he lost favor with Pius XII and was appointed Archbishop of Milan. There, he proceeded to build many parishes that included churches, schools, medical schools, dormitories, and cafeterias. It was an American model as pioneered by Father Tucker at Saint Anthony of Padua in Wilmington, Delaware beginning, under Vatican auspices, in 1924. It was a departure from European conceptions of a parish. In fact, Father Tucker had already shown that the model could be applied in Europe by his success at Saint Charles, Monaco, before Archbishop Montini began his program at Milan.

Father Tucker, then, had the approval of progressive elements at the Vatican based on his proven track record.

Monsignor Tardini, Father Tucker's classmate, was the Pro-Secretary of State for Extraordinary Affairs, a department that handles diplomatic and political affairs. Consequently, Pius XII would assign Monsignor Tardini to handle the Monaco Question. Tardini was aligned with the conservative elements at the Vatican, though more centrist than extreme.

The Tucker approach that made the parish the heart of community or neighborhood life was also popular with the Italian traditionalists. Father Tucker had proven that in Delaware. Consequently, he had the complete support of the Vatican Diplomatic Service. He was "balanced" — supported by both left and right.

The traditionalists (conservatives) took an "at war" approach against Marxism to include and encourage political action. Where feasible, they would encourage alliances between Church and State. They saw in the small principality of Monaco a micro-state that could be an exemplar of effective Church-State cooperation in meeting the religious and social needs of its citizens and residents, while combatting both Communist intrusion and "privileged excess," the reason for Father Tucker saying he was "angry with the surroundings." However, for Monaco to work, the Royal Family itself would have to reflect a Catholic Christian ethic. A single, life-loving Prince just wouldn't do. There would have to be a Princess. But what a woman it would have to be. No wonder Father Tucker said: "I've got a job on my hands, baby!" The kind of woman the Vatican hoped the Prince would find was rare indeed. Without her, scratch Monaco.

◆◆◆

Sept. 16, 1951

Dear Joe:
Bishop McDonnell, Auxiliary of N.Y. and National Director of Propagation of Faith, greeted at Monte Carlo by Gorgeous George Shugrue and World Representative at-large of the OSFS.

He was with 230 pilgrims from 24 states, stayed with us 2 days, celebrated and preached in our Church. Declared that this stop was highlight of trip, and presence of American Oblates in this international center a blessing for the Church and boon for America.

I'm on my way now to preach retreat to Oblates at Marseilles. The French are waking up!

When shall I see you? Here or there?

And when shall I hear from you? Ed? and Helen?

I'm well, sneezing more than you ever did! — and bearing up bravely under the yoke of my harness, the latest contraption being a ball-bearing gear with smooth motion! As Shakespeare said: "My Kingdom for a horse!"

Be good and patient and kind, and grow old gently! We have both already outlived the days of Grandma Hickey.

My love to all!

JFT

✦✦✦

Father Tucker was an exceptional retreat master for both religious and laity. An Oblate retreat lasts 10 days yearly, which time is given to spiritual renewal through prayer, meditation, discussion, rest and isolation from normal duties.

Nov. 22, 1951

My dear Joe:

I'm at the palace waiting for the Prince to call me. It's a strange journey's end for an old trooper of my calibre. My departure was as abrupt as my arrival. I got Samir back to school, and then was kept alerted by TWA for ten hours before take-off. Father Lawless waited all that while to see me off. Father McCoy had also come up to say good-bye. I didn't phone Helen or you or anybody because I was sad enough and tired. Yes, I enjoyed the visit and the lion's share of it I had with you. Will write at length.

The homesickness followed a visit to the USA.

Dec. 5, 1951

Dear Joe:

At this writing, I have received from Father Buckley a Xmas CARE package with turkey and trimmings and already a few cards.

Last evening, the Prince called me to the Palace and said he wanted a midnight mass in the Palace chapel, with the Sovereign Family and guests attending and the Chaplain officiating. It's the first time this has been done. In the past, they have always attended the Cathedral! I was concerned about the Bishop getting sore and sorer, but the Prince was adamant, so what can I do? I have, of course, notified the Vatican, which will say nothing, thus giving consent. The Prince takes such good care of Catholic Schools here and has declared Commies "Off limits" in the Principality, that the Vatican cannot afford to estrange him. Besides, the French Bishop has invited their displeasure by his anti-Italian attitude, which now has become an anti-American one directed against your brother. I'm praying to Mary Hickey Tucker to help her offspring! It might be her way of getting me home to you! So join in the prayers.

Do have a MERRY XMAS! My heart is with you, and all its love for all and to all!

JFT

— 5 —
"My Boy, The Prince of Monaco"
by
J. Francis Tucker

There are no "Dear Joe" letters for the Winter and Spring of 1952. None were likely since Father Tucker made an extensive visit to the United States in the late Spring of that year, returning to Monaco the first days of July. It was a "church business" trip, the specific reasons for which were not a family concern.

While in the United States, Father Tucker wrote an article about the prince as titled above. It appears to be a "for publication" article. Following is the article in first draft, pre-
publication form.

✦✦✦

"Dear Father: Can't you forget that I am a Prince and just treat me as one of your boys?"

May 31st, 1952, marks the 29th birthday of His Serene Highness, Rainier III, Prince Sovereign of Monaco, who wrote me the above note some few months after my appointment to the chaplaincy of his Court and Palace.

The assignment of an American priest to this post caused quite a stir in diplomatic circles, among churchmen and in the populace of Europe, a faint ripple of which spread over the homeland with the release of the news by the Associated Press in February 1951. Conjecture and comment on the appointment ran from suspicion of intrigue on my part and irresponsible departure from nationalist tradition on the part of the youthful Prince, to submissive approval, congratulations and best wishes. When asked by friend or foe: "How did you get the job?," I invariably answered: "It's part of the Marshall Plan!" I had long since come to the conclusion that often the best way to treat troublesome issues and persons is to laugh them off.

The history of my case in the Principality of Monaco was given by a distinguished Protestant friend of mine who signs "D.W.T." to the articles he contributes to the English column of the "NICE-MATIN." In May 1950, he wrote: "It will be a matter for deep satisfaction that H.S.H. Prince Rainier III has expressed a keen desire to develop the importance of Monaco as an international center for conferences on all kinds of subjects. It has to be admitted that its past reputation through-out the world has been mainly associated with its casino, and any move in a more serious direction will meet with wide support. Following the recent visit of the Prince to His Holiness the Pope in Rome, I now learn with special interest of the first actual consequences, which I hasten to pass on to the Catholic members of our local Anglo-American Catholic community. This is the appointment of the Very Reverend J. Francis Tucker, Councillor General of The Oblates of Saint Francis de Sales, to the Church of Saint Charles in Monte Carlo. This gentleman has already arrived among us. He saw active service in France in the first World War as Chaplain with the USA Army at Verdun and elsewhere. His home town is Wilmington, Delaware, where he was founder and pastor of Saint Anthony's Church. He is the first American to enter the Oblate Order. He intends to develop the Anglo-American side of Catholic life in the Principality, and will arrange services and sermons in English. He will be assisted by the Reverend George P. Shugrue, OSFS, an Irish priest from Philadelphia.
D. W. T.

I have at Saint Charles' Church three other curates to complete the international set-up: a Frenchman, a Swiss-German, and an Italian, all members of the Oblate Fathers, to whom the Holy See entrusted Saint Charles' parish of 8000 souls, as D.W.T. said, after the visit to be his chaplain.
This was his privilege, just as it is the privilege of every child of the Church to have his own confessor and spiritual

director, with the difference that his choice results auto
matically in the nomination of the Chaplain to the Royal
Palace, provided always, as in all cases of ecclesiastical
jurisdiction, that the Local Ordinary, the Bishop of Monaco
in the present instance, approves.

The questions still remain: "Why an American?"
And, "Why me?"

To the second question: "Because I was there."

To the first: "Because although French is the official
language in the Principality (and I can make myself understood), English is the household language in the Royal Family.
The young Prince even speaks "American," having been a
liaison-officer in the last war for the French with an outfit from
Texas. One of my spiritual duties is to call him now and then
for the use of certain expressions the cowboys taught him!"

Prince Rainier belongs to the Grimaldi Dynasty that goes
back a thousand years to a Consul of Genoa of that name. The
present Sovereign is the thirtieth descendant in direct line. His
family-tree on the side of his mother, Princess Charlotte,
includes the House of Baden, the Houses of Douglas and
Hamilton of Scotland and England, and, on his father's side,
Prince Pierre de Polignac, one of France's most renowned
Grand Old Families.

Because the Salic Law obtains in Monaco as in England,
Rainier came to the succession through his mother.

Family ties as well as political affinities bring to the Court
of Monaco a stately procession of crowned and uncrowned
dignitaries and world figures of yesteryear and of today. They
find there a resplendent setting, miniature only in size, not in
quality, as dignified in its princely protocol as it is warm with
its welcome from the heart of a wishful "Texan Boy."

It was Prince Rainier's own democratic leanings and
preferences displayed with an ease of manner and engaging
charm that made my debut in such society less painful. A
priest's training in the art of sacred liturgy makes him no

stranger to ceremonial, to bows and reverences, the order of precedence, the exacting gestures and movements required by the strictest of all codes of etiquette, that of the Church. And when such basic training is supplemented by study and practice around the Pontifical Throne of the Papal Court, which was my privilege, the step down from the sanctuary to the worldly arena requires that caution keep alive the consciousness that the priest belongs to a higher level.

Prince Rainier sets the example of showing deference to the spiritual order. To the conventional signs of reverence due to the cloth, he ostensibly adds, with regard to his American chaplain, every indication of deep affection and confidence. Yet, in spite of his note asking me to "treat him as one of (my) boys," I always address him as "My Lord Prince" or "Your Highness," except at rare intervals in intimate conversation. Once, among the many letters he receives from petitioners of favors, stamp-collectors, autograph-hunters, religious cranks and the like, there came one from the USA, addressed to: His Majesty King Charles of Monaco. This furnished us one of these pleasant interludes when I could say to him: "What shall I answer the dope, CHARLIE?," and he said to me, "Whatever your Eminence thinks fit."

It used to annoy him, but now under his chaplain's guidance it amuses him to get letters from lots, especially of the USA, attempting to "save his soul." I tell him of the time when a goodly group of my fellow citizens joined in public prayer for my own conversion simply because I opposed not the Law but the pernicious doctrine of Prohibition. I tell him that he must understand that we Americans are great Law-abiding souls; that, for instance, in my native State of Delaware, because the Law forbids Bingo, that ungodly game of hazard becomes sinful. But happily, by the same token, because the Law sanctions horse racing with pari-mutuel betting, that particular "sport of Kings" makes of the plebeians who follow in the Royal hoofs, virtuous law-abiding citizens. And so, I go on, let *your conscience be at ease, my Lord Prince, because by the very standards of my fellow citizens who busy themselves about the salvation of your impoverished soul, the games at the Casino are NOT sinful because they are sanctioned by the Law.*

The young Prince will allow no one to belittle the Americans. He feels keenly the "bad press." He has too often suffered from the venomous pens of certain scandal-mongering columnists in our "Land of the Free." I remind him that our own Chiefs of State enjoy no immunity from character-lynching, and that because they can withstand such dastardly stabs in the back from soul-thirsty damnationists, it is they, the victims, who make our Country also "the Home of the Brave."

My experience with young men through 43 years in the priesthood makes me KNOW that if my newest ward were lost in the crowd of them without the glitter of his crown, he would not be different from most of them, and much better than many of them.

He likes to dismiss his chauffeur and drive me himself in his car. On one such outing, I spied three U.S. sailors walking alone, and I said to the Prince: "Stop the car and let's call the boys over." He asked why? I told him I wanted to give the boys a thrill by saying: "Fellows, meet the Prince of Monaco!" "I will not!," answered the Prince. "Because I know just what those chaps would reply. They'd say: O'YEA! and I am HARRY TRUMAN!" RAINIER III is never happier than when in the company of Americans. When ships of the Mediterranean Fleet anchor along the Côte d'Azur, he goes all out to arrange for their welcome and pleasant time in the Principality. He will not allow men in uniform or minors in the Casino except for a guided tour of the palatial establishment. They have free entrance to the Palace, the famous Exotic Gardens, and the Oceanographic Museum, and free use of the Royal Stadium.

The Prince gladly accepts invitations to inspect the ships that anchor in the Port of Monaco. I have accompanied him several times on tours of inspection. He keeps among his prized souvenirs a 2 by 3-inch piece of wood, an inch thick, cut from the deck of the U.S.S. MISSOURI, bearing the inscription: "Upon this spot on 7 September 1949 the instrument of formal surrender of Japan to the United States was signed," given him by Admiral Mac Lean abroad the ship. In return for such and similar courtesies, gala receptions are held at the Palace for "Skipper and Staff" with no less ado for plain Mr. American than for the Duke of Edinburgh. At one of these luncheon receptions, I who wear no decoration but my American Legion button, felt inspired to conclude the Grace before meals by adding: "God save the Prince and Principality, and God bless America!" I had overlooked the fact that there were also present a French and a British Admiral. The Prince was delighted that I had pulled a boner. But the Master of Protocol was not pleased. He told the Prince about it, and the Prince said to me: "Next time, Father, just say it in Latin!"

In these circles where Royalty attends, the Masters of Protocol always remind me of wolves in sheep's clothing, or top sergeants in full dress, coat and tails, whose motto seems to be: "Soften the Blow, but Blow!" At a Christmas Party for the Monagasque children given every year in the Palace, the prince's arrival had been delayed. Meanwhile, the hundreds of little ones (limited to 12 years) were being entertained by professional clowns imported from Paris. Without asking leave of the Master of Protocol, I betook myself to the theater of action and was sharing in the glee and laughter and applause of the children when a courier came to claim my attendance on the Prince. I made my way for the stairway to find at the top of the stair Their Serene Highnesses of the Sovereign Family surrounded by members of the Court, all except me, and the Master of Protocol hiding an ugly look under a forced smile. The Prince, who loves to get some goods on his chaplain, was smiling broadly; yet was quick to say: "Father, you are late!" I ventured meekly the reply: "My Lord Prince, it isn't every day that one gets to see clowns!" The Prince grabbed my hand and helped me up the remaining steps with everybody laughing heartily, except the Master of Protocol.

The young Sovereign's father, stately, handsome, erudite Prince Pierre, with consummate good nature and savoir-faire, will drop a word of paternal advice to his illustrious son. I have greatly admired the young Prince's filial devotion to his august parents, and the kindly, considerate way he knows how to combine family and official relationship with them. Once, in my presence, the father in superbly genteel fashion said to the son who had kept both of us waiting for a rendezvous: "Promptitude is the politeness of Kings!" To which Rainier answered: "Dad, we are only Princes!" And I got in the last word: "Don't either of you come late to Mass tomorrow!"

The two Princes did me the honor of coming to Saint Charles rectory for dinner one evening. Never had I seen Their Highnesses more at ease than in the modest company of us five Oblate priests. Our only other guest was a young blind Brother of a French Religious Order. He did most of the entertaining by initiating all of us into the magic of braille. I had asked the Prince to suggest a menu to his liking. We ordered Irish Stew, and we had it. And that was all, with a bit of salad and some dessert. The compliment both father and son paid was to ask if in some way they could not "join the Order."

To his mother, Princess Charlotte, who renounced the succession in his favor, Rainier is as most sons always are to their mothers, "just a teenager." Her Serene Highness loses some of her serenity through worry over the liking her son has for speed in driving a car. She mentioned it to me, so I waited for an opening to advance the maternal complaint. It came one day as the Prince was taking off for a "quick" visit to Paris from Monaco. I said to him: "My Lord Prince, don't you think you better have a blessing before starting off?" He asked me why. I said, "Because your mother worries over the way you speed." He answered: "She gave me a Saint Christopher medal; won't that do?" I said: "Your mother will feel safer if you have the blessing too." He hesitated no longer and, stepping on the gas, he chuckled: "If anything happens, tell Mother I got the blessing!"

Princess Charlotte told me this charming story about her and her boy: One morning she wanted him to go to early Mass with her but Rainier was sleeping, so she let him sleep. Came the afternoon, and Princess Charlotte begged him to accompany her in a visit to a monastery of cloistered nuns. If he came along, she could profit of the privilege accorded only to a reigning Sovereign to enter the enclosure. Rainier weakened to the maternal coaxing and soon found himself alongside his mother, seated in the great chapter-room of the convent, surrounded by the delightful talk about her work and interest in prisons and hospitals. The visit lasted two hours. The punishment had its effect: Rainier said; "Next time, I'll go to Mass!"

As one might expect, it is easier for a son to be "boss" to father and mother, than for a brother to Lord it over his sister, especially when she happens to be two years his senior. Such is the priority that the attractive, lovely Princess Antoinette can claim, and sometimes does, over her Sovereign who happens to be her "little brother."

With other pictures of the Family that adorn Saint Charles Rectory, there is one of Princess Antoinette, which I had a hard time rescuing from a group of sailor boys from the U.S.S. Gearing: "Just think what it would mean to have a Princess for a pin-up girl! Ah! come on, Father, have a heart!?" — all this not from one spokesman but from the whole chorus of what is known in the Navy as "the Fighting Four." This episode pleased Brother all the more for the fact the DD 710 had honored him, and he had honored officers and crew by an exchange of cordial visits and souvenirs.

Princess Antoinette succeeded her mother in sponsoring the Monagasque branch of the International Red Cross. Frequently, she accompanies her brother or substitutes for him at the many functions occasioned by charitable causes, distinguished visitors, sportive events, cultural gatherings, and religious feasts.

Since I am back in the States, I received a letter from the Princess in which, among other things, she asked me to send her some "I like Ike" buttons with a view of distributing them among U.S. citizens abroad. I insert this item not by way of a political "plug," but to show how right the sailor boy was about Antoinette's "Americanism," which quality Her Highness caught by direct contact with the American way of life during an incognito visit to the USA some few years ago.

The American "colony" in the Principality of Monaco is headed by Admiral Nichols who represents the USA on the International Commission of Oceanographic Research, and by Colonel Maynard, one-time United States Consul, now in retirement at Monte Carlo. Recently, I acted as one of three judges at a Prep School debate in which the Colonel's daughter, Joanne, defended the thesis: "Great deeds derive from the heart rather than from the mind." Prince Rainier delights in sponsoring and assisting at such cultural sessions of young and old. Last year the Prince's coveted prize (one million francs) for the outstanding contributor to French literature was awarded to an American, Julien Green.

At present, the interests of United States citizens in the Principality come under the jurisdiction of the U.S. Consul at Nice, which extends to the whole area of the Maritime Alps. Yet for all practical purposes, especially urgent ones, since the advent of American priests to Saint Charles, that spot has become sanctuary and oasis for all our compatriots.

Apart from the enthusiastic pro-American spirit of Prince Rainier, there is a "good neighbor" atmosphere created by the geographic smallness of the Principality which makes Americans feel less like Innocents Abroad. Perhaps Louis Veuillot has found the best expression for it: "If I had the ambition to rule, I would be tempted but by two thrones in the world: that of the Tzar of Russia who rules over 120 million souls, or that of the Prince of Monaco who knows all his subjects by their first name."

◆◆◆

Prince Rainier seems to have been habitually forty minutes late — possibly even at birth. He almost missed meeting Grace Kelly on her visit to his Palace early in 1955. He could joke about it. On their wedding day, he is alleged to have said to Grace that if he was late for the wedding ceremony, she should go on without him.

The Prince served as an intelligence officer with De Gaulle's Army in 1944–45. His awards included the French Croix de Guerre and the American Bronze Star. The Prince was hospitable to NATO armed forces, particularly American, that visited Monaco. But there was one lapse that led to a private, serious confrontation with his chaplain late in 1952 that will be the subject of Chapter 8.

July 8, 1952

Dear Joe:
I had a fine trip in the air, and pleasant arrival in France. Prince Pierre was waiting for me in Paris & had me to lunch. His son, Rainier III, had me at his villa all day July 4th. I visited the Bishop, the cold old frog!
 Came to Rome the 6th; fine reception here from the General & Co. ...
 Am off to Albano today, & then after seeing the Pope tomorrow, shall return to M.C.
 Love to Edna & All
 JFT

This letter evidences the relief the Royal Family felt at having their chaplain back.

— 6 —
"Grandpop" and Other Honors

The assignment of Captain William Taylor and family to Trieste, Yugoslavia in August 1952 allowed Father Tucker to become Uncle Francis in person to niece Betty, with four young children and one on the way. His experience with them in 1952–53 seems to have strengthened his belief in a celibate priesthood. Once more he had a "helluva" time.

His letters to brother Joe from mid-1952 to early 1954 reflect changes in the Catholic hierarchy in Monaco, honors received and work, work, work.

◆◆◆

August 26, 1952

Dear Joe,
Your letter about your vacation was interesting; so was the
$5.00 which eased my conscience into an acquisition of 2 fifths
of Old Lady Gin plus a dollar's worth of snacks for a
foundation, without having to call on Community Funds for
the selfish purpose. I take one Martini a day at evensong and
live all day long in blissful expectation of same. So that your
monthly contribution to the Church on this side of the Kingdom
is held in grateful daily remembrance. Now I look to your
coming to Europe again! The custom here calls for men ap-
pearing in shorts. I have been giving study to the approaching
problem as it will affect you and Harve. My considerate opin-
ion is that the girls, Edna and Hazel, should cut a pair of pants
already made to your waist's measure and roomy about the
thighs. I would say to halfway between knee and buttocks on
the inner side of the knee, and a half-inch more allowance on
the outer side. I find that the ready-made fits over here don't fit
at all, and make one of your and Harve's build and age look
Boy-Scoutish. Whereas the home-made cut is the kindest cut to

all concerned. Black is used at times, but so are striped patterns. The only thing the girls will have to bother about is a veil for their heads for going to church. The priests are particular about this. If they wore any more than this, the natives would think that they belonged to a sect, and would be scandalized.

I hope you arrange to come when the travelling rates are low and when the season is out of season. And of course, 3 months will be required for the absence from home. Certainly Edna must be here shortly, as any good mother would want to be. The Little Sisters of the Poor can always be relied on for old age security, and why wait until then to be secure? It's therefore a go: Hazel and Edna (with veils), and you and Harve (with shorts).

I'll be seeing you! CHEERIO!

◆◆◆

Uncle Francis mixed his own martini with pomp and circumstance. Gordon's Gin was his favorite. Evensong is the period of first Vespers in the Roman Catholic Church, a period of evening prayer and the illumination of a sanctuary by candle light. Whether our dear uncle considered the ritual Martini as part of the "illumination" is speculative.

The Tuckers, Edna and Joe, and the Smuckers, Hazel and Harve, did not make it to Monaco in 1952. Family scuttlebutt has it that when the Pennsylvania Dutchman Harve heard about the shorts, he firmly retired from the project.

◆◆◆

Monte Carlo
Nov. 23, 1952

My dear Joe:
I got Edna's letter of the 10th — so happy to hear from and about you all!

On the 19th, National Holiday of Monaco, the Prince knighted me in the Order of Saint Charles. This is quite a distinction, handed out usually to persons who for a stretch of time, 10 or 20 years, have done notable service to the Principality. It corresponds to a Knight of Saint Gregory in the Papal Court, or Knight of the Garter in the Court of Saint James! The recipient has the right to wear a small red ribbon in the lapel of his coat at all times, and a huge gold medal with a larger ribbon on gala occasions. It carries with it certain privileges and rates salutes and courtesies from Government employees, including traffic-cops. I am sending you photos to confirm all this.

The fact is, and best proof of it: the clerical jealousy and popular approval that abound. The fact is, I say, that we Oblates have done a good job here in many fields of endeavor. We organized the Prince's Cadets (with the old uniforms of North East Catholic I got when home), I got George Shugrue appointed Chaplain of the Monaco High School, and a French Oblate chaplain at the hospital. I'm chaplain of the Palace, and we have this fine parish of Saint Charles.

I don't always get the support one could expect from the OSFS themselves. I mean the French, because like all Frenchmen, they do nothing themselves and want nobody else to do something.

And the struggle against the old bishop goes on! Because he is one hyper-nationalist of the ninth degree, who puts the French cock (a bird) above the Cross on his church-steeples.

I've had a touch of intestinal grippe, the most agonizing phase of it being that I was allowed no such relief as one gets from Southern Comfort, and had to submit to the humiliating diet of stewed carrots without salt, boiled rice with salt, and a baked apple. I said my two masses today, however, and am hanging on, feeling more rabbit than man.

Cheerio! Love to all! Tell the friends about your brother "Cavalier."

JFT

✦✦✦

The knighthood in the Order of Saint Charles came within 21/2 years of Father Tucker's arrival at Monte Carlo — remarkable. The Prince was stingy with such honors. However, Princess Grace was knighted on her arrival for her wedding a few years later.

Evidently, some Frenchmen are truly imaginative in their quest for hyper-nationalism.

Monte Carlo
Jan. 17, 1953

My dear Joe:
I'm disturbed at not having heard from you, and am wondering if it's ditto with you? Sometimes cooks are so bent on getting a start on deserts and side dishes that they neglect the main dish. Could this have been the way with me as regards you and Edna? I had hoped to do some of my Xmas correspondence by way of Father Shugrue. He left on the 15th, and since his departure I have had his work to do, ciphers, and accts, and three masses every Sunday, his Catechism, and youth clinics, including the Prince's band of cadets. All this and my own triple life of parish-priest, Prince's chaplain and Oblate Councillor General.

I went to Rome for 5 days between Xmas and the New Year. Was warmly greeted at the Vatican for what is being achieved at Monaco. The work, the worry, the handicaps are telling on me, and I am weary, after passing my 63rd birthday. I remember that this was Grandma Hickey's age at her death, and surely we thought she was old! The blizzard of 1910.

Time and tide have washed me to the shores of the Mediterranean; it's interesting to outlive one's own wake. Just when I'll rise again in the USA is a question. Father Buckley has invited me to the dedication of the Washington Scholasticate, but this has to pass the General and the Vatican and the Prince and the local Bishop! I too am the servant of the servants of God! Mrs. Dupee wrote her delight at being your guest and seeing the pictures of me blessing dogs! Here are two more solemn ones; being greeted at the stairs by Rainier and his father, and one alone with his father, Pierre de Polygnac! How's Francis? My prayers are always for you and yours!

Love to all!
JFT

♦♦♦

The next letter is the first indication of a change in bishops at Monaco.

Monte Carlo
March 4

My dear Joe:
I got your letter of Feb. 28th, with news clippings, and 1,970 francs, a substantial help to my multiple needs. The Democrat's Act of Resignation I showed to the Prince, who kept it! As to the news, although blue, it was just what I wanted to know about the people I'm interested in. ... Joe McCoy sent me a cable about K. Bowe's death. She was the most trustworthy and trusted of my female admirers, outside the family of course. The only one I think that Mother T. never got jealous of, Kathryn both by nature and by grace was cold. There's no question but that her place is among the virgins.

I'm preaching the LENTEN course here at Saint Charles to

packed audiences. They always had the Bishop before, but the old bastard refused to come this year, so I boldly met the challenge. He is being relieved of his duties and blames me for it, not without reason. The Prince presented my name to the Holy Father for the succession. The Papal reply was couched in fatherly terms of esteem of my merits, but went on to say that a younger man was what they had in mind. And, in fact, the Prince referred to me the proposed candidate, a fine French-man (rare to find), 46 years old. The truth is, of course, that the French Government interposed. It has a right of assent due to its Concordat with the Holy See on Alsace and Lorraine because this Principality, although independent, has agreements with the French Government that are far-reaching.

Well, I got that far, anyhow, Joe, and it's been a lot of fun. They all know that TUCK has been around. It's incredible how nationalistic the French are. Our own OBLATES, the FRENCH, didn't want to see a non-Frenchman get it, albeit a confrere. Yet the Prince's and the Vatican's tribute to me, both in writing, of which I retain copies for the archives, is more than any French Oblate ever got or ever will get for the Congregation.

On Ash Wednesday, a package you sent me arrived with a ten-dollar tax slapped on it by the French customs, without opening it. They would not let me open it, so I had it returned. The truth is I didn't have that kind of money to shell out at this time, and I had got burnt once before for a package of old used toys someone sent for the kids over here. What was it you sent me? I'm curious to know and whether it was returned.

I'm off to tea with Prince Pierre and the Consul from Bolivia. It's a hell-of-a-life, and to think I'm leading it all for the love of God! ...

I wrote the Divine girls and Bill at Xmas. Never a word, much less a stingy French franc!

Cheerio!

JFT

✦✦✦

In 1953, the agreement, Quemodmodum, between Vatican and Principality was still operative.

The Prince had the privilege of participating in the selection of clergy who would serve in the diocese of Monaco. Father Tucker did participate in the selection of a new bishop, the Most Reverend Giles Barthe. Quemodmodum was replaced by a new agreement in 1982, in which the Prince gave up all privilege in the selection of clergy for Monaco. In return, Monaco was elevated to the status of archdiocese, headed by an archbishop. Some day there may be a Cardinal at Monaco.

July 20, 1953

Dear Joe:

I've been here over a week to give a report on outgoing and incoming Bishops. Seems I did a good job in both instances. The first official act of the new Bishop was to name me Canon of his Cathedral, the worth of which lies principally in the vindication given me over old Bishop Riviere's opposition to me. Here at the Vatican this gesture was well received. ...

I'll return tomorrow to M.C. Thanks again for the Heraldry — great stuff indeed!

Love to Edna & All

(Canon) JFT

Right Reverend Canon Tucker! One "n"

✦✦✦

A canon is a member of the chapter of a cathedral or collegiate church. The bishops of America do not appoint canons. Recognition of outstanding service by a male clergyman is given by designation as a monsignor with its privileges. Evidently, canon is a step above monsignor.

Of all the honors and awards Father Tucker received, the appointment as Canon appears to be the one he most cherished. He was pleased to be known as Canon Tucker — the Right Reverend Canon Tucker.

Father Tucker's niece, Betty, and family went to Rome in August with the Canon joining them there, as his next letter shows.

Aug. 22

Dear Joe:
Have spent so far 2 days <u>here</u> with Betty, Bill, Mrs. Taylor, Billy, Dick, Barbara, Betsy, and I am half-dead and willing to die completely! Your grandchildren insisted on calling me "Grandpop" this time! 'Twas embarrassing in Vatican circles and in the fashionable English Tea Shop, where Betsy went into a tantrum. We were 3/4-hour with the Pope in general audience yesterday. The kids were fine. Were kept that way by a promise I made that the Holy Father would give them ice cream if they were good. I'm afraid their tender faith in Papal infallibility is wrecked for life! I'm off with them to Mass now. The visits to the Basilicas were a success via orangeade & cone after each stop.
 Love to Edna!
 Got your Anniversary card and cards from Colorado!
 JFT

✦✦✦

It is alleged that uncle Francis told Betty that if Pius XII had to baby sit her children for an afternoon, he should no longer advocate large families.

"Grandpop" provided a large car with an Italian chauffeur and Italian guide to tour the Eternal City. Betsy raised the temper tantrum to an art form, attracting sizable audiences at the 7 hills tea house, the steps of Saint Peter's Basilica, and several other locales. She fell asleep on the floor of the car at one point. Uncle Francis shouted "Don't touch her, don't touch her" when her brother Billy tried to arouse her. Ice cream cones were provided after each stop. A successful goodwill gesture.

The audience with the Pope was at his summer residence, Castel Gondolfo. The guide arranged for them to have the "window" for the Pope's appearance on the Veranda. Uncle Francis said to Betty's husband, Bill, "Give this guy $20 in American money." Bill said "I don't have American money, only lira and military paychecks."

"So give him (the guide) $20 in lira then," which he did. The children were in awe of Pius XII, behaving well throughout.

Uncle Francis then drove them to the Rome zoo, let them out and said, "I'm going home." His peace and quiet were brief. The Taylor tribe decided to visit Monaco late in August.

Betty was eager to meet with Princess Antoinette. They had corresponded and exchanged family pictures since the Taylors arrived in Trieste. As Betty recalls, Father Tucker was very fond of Princess Antoinette and her children. He was helpful to her, particularly as a family mediator, for her relationship with her brother was often strained at that time. He spoke to the Princess about his niece and a correspondence began. Uncle Francis made arrangements for them to stay at a hotel on the water. Their outings included dinners, movies, beach and sightseeing.

The Big Event was a visit to the Princess and her children. Uncle Francis was like a "hen on a hot griddle." He was afraid the Taylor kids would beat up the three beautiful royal children — a girl, 7; a boy, 6; and a girl, 2. Prior to the visit, he instructed them on protocol, including how to bow.

No problems — except him. The royal children spoke English. The Princess — "a good looking doll" according to Bill, but more appropriately, a beautiful woman — explained that the children would learn French in school. Her children were dressed in boxer shorts with no tops. All played beautifully together with the royal toys that included a large walk-in doll house. Hors d'oeuvres were served by an English-speaking butler. The ladies visited amidst it all. They parted as friends, exchanging notes and Christmas cards for several years. Uncle Francis was surprised, pleased and relieved, and, one suspects, privately renewed his vow of celibacy even though of age 64.

Betty and Bill recall an evening reception at the rectory to which they were invited. The rectory has two large dining rooms. The men were in one, Betty and children in the other. Not too pleased, but she did avoid the cigar smoke and other forms of air pollution.

The Prince was away at this time.

✦✦✦

25 Sept. 53

My dear Joe:
You remember without doubt our visit here. I came back to the
scene of my youthful Roman days to give and make a retreat.

Since the Taylor tribe visit to Monte Carlo, I have literally
not had a moment to myself. Correspondence filled up
shamefully & discouragingly. But what's the use?

I wanted so much to tell Edna how proud I was of Betty
before Princess Antoinette! If anything Betty was more
Princess than the titled-one. Antoinette seemed conscious of it.

This summer has been a hectic one for me. Father
Shugrue's departure left me, among other souvenirs, the many
visitors he magnanimously invited to come to Saint Charles. I
hope to save a few francs now that my dollar-man is back in
the land of dollars. I went to Turin with the new Bishop — in
quality of Canon, have been to Lourdes, and now touring our
houses in Italy, while the General is in Africa!!! Thank God!
Pray for me!

Love to all,
JFT

The brief mention of a trip to Lourdes prompts comment on two events in 1953 that were important in Prince Rainier's forming a vision of the kind of woman to seek to be both wife and princess.

In mid-1953, Madame Gisele Pascal, Rainier's intimate companion for six years, took the initiative in ending their relationship by moving to Paris. She met Gary Cooper and they became friends. That friendship convinced Prince Rainier that their relationship was over.

Family lore has this account. Prince Rainier was unconvinced that Gisele would not return. When word reached Monaco of the Gary Cooper liaison, it fell on Father Tucker to tell the Prince since no one else would dare. The Prince said "I don't believe it." Father Tucker said, "Come with me to Paris to see for yourself." The Prince agreed. In Paris, the two went to a fashionable Parisian restaurant where they found

Gisele and Gary together.

The meeting was cordial but final. Rainier knew she was gone. Good old Gary!

Father Tucker and Mademoiselle Pascal had no conflicts. She is on record as saying that her relationship with him was cordial and that he was the only one who would tell her the truth. And we know of nothing derogatory that Father Tucker said about her. In fact, he seemed to respect her, recognizing that she was a stabilizing influence on the life of what might have been a wild young man if she were not with him.

About Lourdes! With Gisele gone, the Prince's attention could be directed towards considering the sacramental nature of marriage and the need to find a woman who could enter freely into a sacramental union. One approach was through prayer. A family account is that Father Tucker suggested a trip to Lourdes. The Prince agreed, but as part of the bargain, Father Tucker would agree to accompany him to a ball game. The Prince, one of his close male friends, and Father Tucker drove to Lourdes, an experience that our dear uncle found more life threatening than driving with Father George Shugrue.

The ball game turned out to be a bullfight that triggered an Anglo-Saxon response from the priestly quarter.

This trip may have been in conjunction with a pilgrimage to Lourdes by 600 Monacoans.

✦✦✦

Oct. 25

Dear Joe and Edna:
Thanks for your letter and news clippings duly received, with appreciated enclosure.

'Twas nice of Father Buckley to pinch hit for me at Cousin Margaret's funeral. He sent me the stipend ($10) that Mealey insisted on giving him, Margaret having bequeathed this for the services.

She and Nell Tucker, the milliners on King Street, were delightful spinsters, as far as my innocence of such things allows. Nell was a step ahead of her day on paint and powder, as my childhood memory recalls, sort of a forecast of what our other cousin, Sophie Tucker, was to enliven a dull world with.

I've often thought it a loss of time for the Creator to have made Betty so beautiful, not to have had the asset put to family profit without the expense of paint and powder.

True, Betty's mother could have competed in a Miss America contest were it not for the McJilton puritanism. And Hazel could have run a sure bet for Miss Universe.

There are lost chances that one wakes up to, too late. Harve and yourself might share responsibility in the common loss.

If life retains me in its grip, I intend to cooperate in advancing the prospects of my grandnieces along these hereditary lines, if only to help the Propagation of the Faith. The end justifies the means.

I have heard nothing of Ace or Cliff or their tribes. I do hope Betty sent Princess Antoinette a Sears Roebuck catalogue, which Her Highness asked for. Perhaps her mother might ask her about this for me.

My experiences with the third and fourth generations that bear your trade-mark are harassing, to put it mildly, especially since the Vatican episode on demand of ice-cream from the Pope. I don't dare write them for fear they might come again. Of course, Phyllis' children, with a bit of Protestant restraint, might ask for less. And what about Joe's and Mary's? Or are they cowboys? I get distracted in my prayers thinking of the possibilities, and the adventures of their Grandfather under Western skies. If you and Edna do come over here, please live your age.

I don't think I'll get over this year. The Prince's proposed visit has been held up by elections and protocol requirements for a Sovereign. Then, I'm tired and weary of this life at Court which becomes more and more onerous for me because, owing to the Prince's confidence, I become more each day the man behind the throne. Our Queen Mother never imagined this when she sat me on a pot. Nor did Mother Mac when she fed

*me her hot biscuits. God love them all and us in time and
eternity.*

   Cheerio!
   JFT

This letter probably was written in 1953. Betty did send Princess
Antoinette a Sears Roebuck catalogue.

Father Tucker was a "reluctant Richelieu" at best. The Prince found
that Father Tucker could provide him with pertinent explanations of
many topics, not just religious ones. He was supportive and not a "yes
man." And he was one of the brightest men in Monaco.

Nov. 8

My dear Joe:
*I sent you some photos by Father Bugliosi, one of my fine
Italian boys whom I rescued from the perils of the native
clergy! Get Edna to invite him and Robert for dinner some day.
My diary records: Oct. 24, tea with Princess Charlotte at 5 in
Paris. Oct. 29, 10 a.m. with Bishop of Monaco, noon with
French Consul General; 5 p.m. with Prince Rainier, Princess
Antoinette, Princess Gislaine, and Court. Nov. 4, with Bishop
at Saint Charles at 10 for patronal feast, mass at Palace at 11,
dinner with Bishop at 1. Nov. 7, tea at 5 with Princess
Antoinette in her villa. Nov. 11, at cemetery with Legion. Nov.
15, lunch with Madame Carrol of Carrolton and Prince Pierre.
Meanwhile Dr. Solamito is injecting my ass with anti-virus-
infection gun shots and spraying my throat with electron! After
which I sneak a glass of Gordon's gin just to keep the old
man-of-war in the race! I was never so homesick! Mary Hickey
Tucker appears to me every night, pointing towards heaven!*

   Love to all!
   JFT

✦✦✦

In between the fun he tried to get his work done. Father Tucker had a lifelong history of nasal infections and related distress. A small atomizer was a constant companion. Many of his letters refer to the flu or some other ailment. It seems that he caught a cold on every trip to America. A current explanation would be that his life was too stressful. A reply could be that without stress, he would have had no life.

Monte Carlo
Sunday, Jan. 24, 1954

My dear Joe:
Since the holidays, I've been through devious ways that led to and from Rome, and to and from a bed of sickness, the flu, bad enough to require a Doctor, and an amiable though ugly-to-look-at old nurse, who surely got more pleasure than I out of sticking needles in my ass. For 10 days I've been cooped up, but did say mass early this morning, and now waiting the Dr. in hopes of getting loosed from the bondage of plaster and pills, which over here are always accompanied by carrots and boiled rice.

I got a card from Frankfurt with no address! What is it? I wanted to go there during the holidays, and perhaps if I had, I would have escaped the grippe I got here. And Cliff? I would like to know where they are, what is their address, I have a note from Princess Antoinette for Betty. ...

♦♦♦

The Taylors were transferred to Germany late in the Fall of 1953. Betty's brother, Cliff, an Army officer, was also in Germany with his family.

Feb. 18, 1954

My dear Joe:
The Consul General of France announced yesterday that the
French Government has awarded me the Cross of the Legion of
Honor. It's a real distinction and, in my case, a victory for an
American priest in a French parish!
  I'm happy about it and grateful!
  Love to all!
  JFT

◆◆◆

The award was for his work among the French citizens of Monaco
through the parish of Saint Charles at Monte Carlo. Betty's husband,
Bill, attended the presentation of the award at the French legation by
the French consul, a good friend of Father Tucker. A sumptuous dinner
followed. Yankee Vaudeville, indeed. What fools the press can be.

— 7 —
Friends

The friendship between Prince and Chaplain was deep enough to survive a few battles that helped clarify their relationship. In a sense, they were Comrades-in-Arms bound together by a common mission — the spiritual, social and economic development of the Principality. However, for two strong men of differing social backgrounds, each with a sense of his own "turf," not to have had a few lovely fights (as the Irish might say) was unlikely. All that was needed was the occasion. One arose on December 26, 1952.

His Serene Highness
Rainier !!!
PRINCE OF MONACO

My dear Lord Prince:
The enclosed copy of a letter which I was obliged by sheer decency to send to Commodore Pilkington before the departure of his ships from this port is self-explanatory.

I am of course convinced that your Highness did not foresee the impact that yesterday's complete let-down at the Palace would necessarily have.

May I refresh your memory on this matter.

You told me to confer with Father Shugrue on this sort of thing to do for these sailors. I reported to you our joint conclusion. You went so far as to tell me how I should call for you in your office, and you would come informally to greet the men. I had so briefed the Commander, who in turn had briefed the men.

And now may I tell you a few reactions to the misunderstanding, or whatever it was:

Father Shugrue and I were made to look not only silly and foolish, but belittled before our compatriots and the personnel of your place. Father Shugrue's reaction: "It's on account of you, Father Tucker, that I stay here. When I see you slapped in the face, I quit! And when I see our American boys, who spent their holidays trying to make happy kids of Monaco, insulted as nowhere else or ever before, I also quit. Because, no matter what explanation is given, this is unpardonable."

Commander Pilkington's reaction: "Let's forget we were ever at Monaco!"

Colonel Severac's reaction: "Father, I am sorry for you, and I feel sorry for the Prince."

My own reaction: "I cannot quit. I can take a slap in the face. But I shall not turn the other cheek!"

It may be, my Lord Prince, that because there are so many unprincipled persons in your circle that you think all men are made of the same stuff. Such stuff is not made in the USA.

Sincerely,

That this happening was a public relations "gaffe" by the Prince is obvious. Father Tucker moved immediately to damage control by a letter to Commodore Pilkington (copy not available) and a strong letter to the Prince that among other things said, don't let it happen again. That letter launched a 3-day war between Prince and Chaplain.

Father Shugrue meant what he said. He left Monaco within 3 weeks, evidently without pardoning the Prince. He left disenchanted with "the playing with religion" of many in theRoyal coterie and their worship of status over accomplishment. He was a working class American.

And what did the Prince do? He wrote back in his own hand. The following are excerpts from the Prince's letter.

"I am, Father, very surprised and extremely shocked by the terms of your letter dated December 27th."

He then wrote "his side of the story," indicating that he had been very tired and expected to be awakened to attend an informal but not official meeting with the sailors and stated that he was offended by the tone of his chaplain's letter.

"May I remind you <u>that you are at my service</u> and by your functioning as chaplain you should have ... I thought and hoped that you were near enough to me to speak about things."

He concluded with "I thought (and think of you perhaps still) as not <u>an American</u> but as my official chaplain of no nationality."

I remain as ever yours faithfully,

Prince Rainier

◆◆◆

Well, Uncle, how did you like that?

If there was a question as to whether Prince Rainier really believed himself to be absolute monarch, this letter answers it. He did, though he relented to some degree in the revision of the Monacoan Constitution, 1962.

This letter should silence those who said that Father Tucker had a Rasputin-like control over Prince Rainier. He did not ever. The Prince was a firm and determined young man for whom Father Tucker was a trusted friend and advisor.

Perceptive comments about the Prince provide some insight about his character.

"He is a true Gemini with a Mediterranean culture."

"Gemini, a twin-sided person. A Mediterranean who can explode with anger, but in a minute all is forgotten, and the recipient of the wrath is bathed in unconditional bonhomie. And, like all Mediterranean men, the Prince can be unreasonably jealous."

"He used to be shy, somewhat introverted, occasionally melancholic. Public appearances have never ceased to be an ordeal for him."

Perhaps that is a slight clue as to why he did not appear to greet the American sailors. The Prince did end his letter with "yours faithfully."

In any case, dear Uncle, the "ball is in your court." Are you going to be a "Yes Man?"

◆◆◆

28 December, 1952

HIS SERENE HIGHNESS
RAINIER III
PRINCE OF MONACO

My Lord Prince:

*In deference to Your Highness' reaction to my letter of the 27th
inst., as written in Your hand in a letter delivered to me by
courier this day, December 28th, I respectfully submit to Your
Highness my resignation as chaplain of the Palace, to become
effective at Your Highness' pleasure.*

*Your Highness' reaction, if I understand rightly, bespeaks
an attitude that requires of me for a continuance in Your
Highness' service:*

*First, a renunciation of the character and prerogatives of
an American citizen.*

*Second, submission of my views on Christian ethics and
values to views that I consider erroneous.*

*If I misinterpret Your Highness' written word, I shall
welcome an exchange of the spoken word with You at Your
Highness' convenience.*

*Meanwhile, I shall continue to cherish the remembrance of
the grateful acknowledgement Your Highness recently made in
writing to the Holy See of the accomplishments effected by the
Oblate Fathers, since April 1950, in favor of Your August
Person, Your Sovereign Family and Your People of the
Principality.*

*For all of You, regardless of such disposition as may be
made of me, I shall continue to hold a lasting true and sincere
priestly affection.*

Devotedly Yours,

Hell, No, I'm not going to be a Yes Man! I quit, if I can. This letter
was the official, for the record, Oblate response. It was accompanied
by an "unofficial footnote" that reads like the Uncle Francis we knew.

28 December, 1952

My Dear Boy, My very dear Rainier:
*As a footnote to the enclosed official letter, I added this
personal written word to clear up a few matters with you:*

*You should tell Me: "Beware of writing!" Boy Oh Boy!
Does the kettle call the pot black? I write purposely, to study
my words, and to offset misquotation.*

Then, you tell me what I should have done: "Phone, etc."

*I did phone, or rather Severac phoned for me, in presence
of the Commander, and the answer was precisely what You
suggested: "The Prince is delayed!" But some people can't fall
for that stuff. Some people think that You should have phoned:
"I won't be there," or given orders to wake you up for your
appointment.*

*Here's where our code of ethics differs! You dismiss the
whole thing as "Unimportant!" You say the visit was carried
out as scheduled. It was NOT. The whole raison d'etre of the
visit centered around YOU! The boys put so much importance
on it that they gave up their shore-leave and coughed up dough
to charter the buses.*

*... It doesn't matter to me that the boys were Americans, in
spite of Your nasty crack about Your anti-American help! If they
were Hindus, or Hottentots, or Monagasques (I can be nasty
too), it's all one: it's a question of human dignity and what
price you put on it.*

*When you say I'm "childish" and "act like a girl," I feel
like saying "You're another!" What more girlish than to say
"I'll remember!" In America, the phrase is: "I'll get even with
you!" and that evidently is what you mean, and that's what
burnt me up. I'll be damned if I'll go around that Palace with
your pouting and "remembering" Or should I say: "That
scares me to death!?"*

*When you say that you don't think of me as an American,
you're the winner of First Prize in the International Liars'
Club, Inc., plus your brushing off of Father George's just
wrath, equal only to your own over a foul play.*

*The payoff is your remark about my absence from your
Xmas party! Well! I didn't think it was "important." Nor was I
going to expose myself to get a Princely kick in the ass from a*

guy who has a memory like an elephant.

Your very hatred for me proves that you love me. I have never hated you and never will. I'll keep on telling you the truth even if it hurts.

God bless you!

Your Ex-chaplain,

That seemed to cover everything. Ex-chaplains can tell it like it is. In this letter, Father Tucker departed from the formalistic writing style required in royal communications.

Evidently, the Prince did not respond nor did he talk about it with its sender.

The silence prompted another letter from Father Tucker.

5 Janvier, 1953
H.S.H. RAINIER III

My Lord Prince:

Am I to interpret your silence as giving consent to my resignation, or as another notice that You attached no importance to it?

I cannot in good grace retract the resignation, since it was submitted in deference to Your reaction to my letter of 27th December, and made effective only at Your Highness' pleasure.

It was at Your Highness' pleasure and request that I accept the chaplaincy not as a hired servant, but on an honorary basis, through regard, esteem and affection for You, with a view to help a young Catholic Prince, and with no ulterior selfish interests or ambitions.

It never occurred to me that my gratuitous service could one day be commandeered to the point of forfeiting an innate sense of human dignity and the honor of a gentleman.

Yet this is what happened on December 27th in the opinion of all persons involved in or acquainted with the treatment that I received at Your hands on that date.

Then followed Your letter adding insult to injury. You attach "No importance" to the whole affair. ... You accuse me of acting "childish" for not phoning You, when I did phone through Colonel Severac, in presence of Commodore Pilkington and his Aide, and I did say that "the Prince was detained." But certain people are not childish enough to accept such an excuse when they think that it was up to You to do the phoning. Gentlemanly behavior is not restricted to "official or formal" occasion, according to the accepted Code of Christian Ethics and values that obtains in this era of modern civilization.

Your letter follows with the statement that You find Yourself "mistaken" in my regard, and continues with the threat: "I'll remember!"

What am I supposed to do under these two indictments?

Continue in Your service as one You mistrust and as one upon whom will visit a revengeful memory?

I simply can't do this.

I wish to remain in Your services and, as I have often said, I shall not leave of my own accord. It is evident from what you have written that I have become persona non grata in Your sight, which means that I consider myself dismissed. Unless otherwise advised by You, I shall consider it as a fait accompli.

Your dear Mother has just sent me a word of thanks for my Xmas present "with much love!" No Sovereign Order can sever the ties of affection that bind me to Her and Her Son, as much as some smooth friends connive to see this happen.

There is no record of a written response from the Prince. No doubt, prince and priest reconciled in person. Father Tucker remained as chaplain and Ex-chaplain for the next 10 years.

The interchange in these letters was private.

The Prince wrote by hand; the chaplain did his own "hunt and peck" typing.

The incident itself was an isolated one. Prince Rainier, prior to it and afterwards, welcomed American servicemen hospitably. In fact, with his encouragement, Father Tucker served as an Ecclesiastical Chaplain for American military when in the Principality of Monaco. Copies of appointment paper are presented here.

Military Ordinariate
United States of America
30 East Fifty-First Street
New York 22, N.Y.
August 3, 1959

Very Reverend J. Francis Tucker
8, Avenue Saint-Charles
Monte Carlo, Monaco

Dear Father Tucker:
In virtue of the authority granted to me by His Eminence, Francis Cardinal Spellman, Military Vicar, I hereby appoint you as an Ecclesiastical Auxiliary Chaplain of the Military Vicariate.

You are hereby granted all the faculties of the Military Vicariate except those pertaining to marriage. The facilities granted are those outlined in <u>The Vademecum For Priests Serving In The Military Vicariate Of The United States Of America</u> and the <u>Supplement</u> thereto and any other publications as may amend or replace these. These facilities may be utilized in behalf of any subject of the Military Vicar.

You are not granted a personal parochial jurisdiction as the Commissioned Chaplain. In the event you are called upon to handle any marriage, specific delegation for this marriage should be obtained from the Chaplain who has personal parochial jurisdiction or the local civilian Pastor.

This appointment as an Auxiliary Chaplain will perdure until revocation by the Military Vicar or one of his Chaplain Delegates.

Wishing you continued success in your priestly tasks,
I am Sincerely yours in Christ,
Chaplain Delegate

✦✦✦

Military Ordinariate
United States of America
30 East Fifty-First Street
New York 22, N.Y.
June 16, 1955

The Commanding Officer
U.S. Military Establishments in the
Principality of Monaco

Dear Sir:
We have appointed the bearer of this letter, the Reverend <u>J.</u>
<u>Francis Tucker, OSFS,</u> of <u>Monte Carlo, Monaco</u>, as an auxil-
iary chaplain to serve the Catholic personnel under your
command in the absence of a Catholic chaplain.
*   We commend him to your good offices, and we trust that he*
may be given such access to the military areas as may be
necessary for the performance of his spiritual duties.
*   Respectfully submitted,*
James H. Griffiths
Auxiliary Bishop
Chancellor

✦✦✦

Military Ordinariate
United States of America
30 East Fifty-First Street
New York 22, N.Y.
June 16, 1955

Very Reverend J. Francis Tucker
8, Avenue Saint-Charles
Monte Carlo, Monaco

Dear Father Tucker:

In virtue of the authority granted to me by His Eminence, Francis Cardinal Spellman, Military Vicar, I hereby appoint you as an Ecclesiastical Auxiliary Chaplain of the Military Ordinariate with <u>full parochial power</u> over all subjects of the Military Ordinariate, who are or will be present at U.S. MILITARY ESTABLISHMENTS AND SUBJECTS OF THE MILITARY ORDINARIATE IN THE PRINCIPALITY OF MONACO.

At the above establishment, the persons subject to your jurisdiction will be <u>Catholics</u> of the following groups:

a) Men of the Armed Forces in active military service, even though they have residence outside the military area;

b) Their wives, children, parents, and servants residing in the same house with them;

c) Civilians staying within the military area; and

d) Religious men, Sisters and lay people, who are attached to military hospitals.

It is to be noted that your appointment is <u>limited to the military post or establishments mentioned above</u> and another appointment issued by this office will be necessary for any other post or establishment.

Your appointment as an Ecclesiastical Chaplain will perdure until revocation by the Military Vicar or one of his delegates, your resignation, your transfer or removal from the parish or other ecclesiastical establishment to which you are

*now assigned by your own ecclesiastical superior. You are,
therefore, requested to notify us immediately of any transfer
from your present ecclesiastical assignment.*

*Praying that you will enjoy your work with the men and
that God will bless your labors with great fruit, I am*

Sincerely yours in Xto.,
James H. Griffiths
Auxiliary Bishop
Chancellor

♦♦♦

In February 1955, Canon Tucker wrote a "long and ecclesiastical"
letter to Prince Rainier about matters Monacoan (copy not available).
What followed were two personally typed letters by Rainier and a first
draft of a formal response by Canon Tucker. The letters are reproduced
here only to show prince and priest in action when in conflict. The
writer is in no position to discuss the issues.

Dear Father,
*I got your long and ecclesiastical letter. Many thanks for this
and that! I fear you have grown a bit tired of your title and
functions? That you are weary of this Palace and its spirit and
atmosphere. You are probably sick to death of me! For all this
I well understand you. And far from giving you hell for this, ...
I am quite sad and astonished! — tout cela n'est pas grave.*

*It's, I suppose, just that the USA can't seem to keep the
position and hold the point!!! Yes for if you neglect the slight-
est, you well know who moves in? All this is taking place slowly
and I can see it slowly growing.*

*Saint Charles — that is the sore spot! Yes, you may well
frown and try to look astonished — there is the truth.*

*You got rid of Father George. He was not a pearl, but he
got things moving. I just have to think of the cadets; they were
better off in his time! Now they are practically on their own.*

That's no good; you know it.

You got Father Joe, a nice kid, but what does he do to help? Not much, and he is less active than old George was! And worse still, you cannot give him much to care for — not even the kids!

So now what? Well you had better get moving so as to get someone effective in to help you at Saint Charles — somebody you can depend on and that will put a bit of life in it all with you. But please don't leave things as they are, and let's stop whimpering.

I got the pack of correspondence from the USA I had given you. Are they all there and ready to be answered? Of course, I realize I made quite a mistake in giving these over to you for reading and project answering; it is not a priest's job, firstly, and secondly, you haven't the time.

Sorry to have troubled you. It was my mistake. There is no harm done, as I have someone who has all the time and who is practically specialized in this kind of work.

May I now, without seeming to overestimate my privilege or power, point out that I was rather shocked to read this in your letter. "It is a summons for me to go to Rome, and I am leaving tonight."

You used to say "can I ... do you mind ... if Your Highness does not need me ... would it be of any trouble if I went to Rome ... and will be back ..."

Well, I suppose those were the days!!! I preferred that way of taking off than this last fashion!

Times change, don't they? And so do all men, even those devoted to Holy matters!!!

I guess you might take this letter badly? That will not be my fault, for I wrote it quite in frankness as I always do.

Affectionately yours,

✦✦✦

INSTITUTUM
Oblatorum S. Francisci Salesii

My Lord Prince:
The General Council in session today considered Your
Highness' complaints as forwarded to me in Your letter
of February 25th.

We all share unanimous regret at Your Highness' displea-
sure, all the more because it is in such contrast with the very
favorable report recently given here in Rome by the Bishop of
Monaco on the Oblates' achievements for the good of religion
in the diocese.

The chaplaincy at the palace, the chaplaincy at the lycee,
the chaplaincy at the hospital, the direction of the Cadets, and
other supplementary services are activities aside from the
original assignment and were accepted in deference to Your
Highness' pleasure. And are carried on by way of a favor to the
diocese, some of them, including the services of Father Bowler,
without financial obligation on the part of the Government.
The Oblates are happy to do this, even at a sacrifice of extra
personnel taken from other fields of their extensive labors.

The American Provincial has been very generous in this
regard. Unfortunately, the matter of displacing priest-educators
from established positions in the different provinces to assume
new occupations is something the Provincials cannot always
afford to do. The withdrawal of Father Shugrue caused all of us
regret, none more than to myself, yet this General Council in
accord with his Provincial felt obligated to do this for the good
of all concerned, primarily for Father George himself. The
Council incidentally regrets his interferences recently in a
private affair of Your Princely Family. This shows, among other
things, how a man's good qualities are often unbalanced by
other considerations. We wished to show another picture of an
American Oblate, especially to our French brethren, and so we
chose Father Bowler. I have the impression that Princess

Antoinette appreciates his dependable and sustained interest in sharing an important responsibility that is hers. Permit me to say that I consider this more important than acting as policeman to the Cadets. I think it a good thing to get these boys into the American habit of behaving according to the honor system and by self-government. There are old boys among them now who can exercise control. Besides, Your Highness has agreed that important progress has been made in the line of music. What they need is for the Carabiniers to train the trumpets, and one to drill them for marching. If the Carabiniers took them under their wing, it would be a hundred times better than if Oblates did.

May it please Your Highness to accept this communication in the spirit of loyal and devoted deference in which the Oblates address it to You.

Father General suggests that I respectfully call Your attention to the fact that the original assignment given five years ago by the Holy See to the Oblates at Monaco was the performance of parochial duties at Saint Charles.

❖❖❖

Dear Father,

So at least, your heart has opened and let forth all it has held back and suffered during these last five years of pain and such deep and continuous suffering!

And what an ugly mess all this is! So since five years you have endured all this with a smile and the nice ways and doings towards me advising me and even encouraging me to go on, and fight my way through. So all this was really a show, and in the bottom of your heart, you really thought I was what you write today?

Five years of silent criticism! That was of no help to me and of no use. If you had come out with what you had on your chest even two years ago, that would have been doing right to me, *and even if it had hurt me then, it would have been better than waiting for the overflow!*

No, really you deceive me, Father! I thought you wanted me good and that from the start, till now? If it had been thus, I would have expected that you would tell me everything you heard, thought or felt, good or bad. Instead, no, the silence and the smile — the facade — until the time comes for you to quietly and scenically tell me that I am some kind of failure and a growing fast MONSTER. Thanks. If that is a way to help, or serve, the people one says one loves, I prefer all should hate me. And if I asked you, your smiling answer would be undoubtedly — "My dear Prince one does not hate you!!!"

As for this uncatholic principality and the horror it does stir in your heart. You are one of God's soldiers, and this is the first time you tell me of this situation! How comes that your vigilance has not been wakened earlier!!! So I drift towards the inevitable, impending CATASTROPHE!!! What a piece of news! What — how — and which — or is it too soon to answer these questions?

I continue to wonder and not understand this sudden change in you, or still less your latest explanation: five years of patient endurance. No, dear Father, this is neither excuse nor explanation. Anyway, I do not hold it valuable for either, because I think it unworthy and sterile to sit through five years, enduring patiently, and not saying a word to the principal interested — myself. "Your boy" as I once was called by you!

I may add today the "boy" you despised — and have now learned to hate or detest!!!

I'm sorry and deceived! It's hard to realize mistakes — and mistakings. But, as I told you, I remain, for keepsake and for any old age.

Affectionately yours

What a lad that young Prince was. He has not been one to back down. He has stood up to Prince Louis, his grandfather whom he succeeded, his strong-willed sister, the Monagasque National Assembly, Onassis, Charles De Gaulle, and the Church itself in the person of Canon Tucker, a Vatican diplomat.

In this exchange, Canon Tucker has shown that he considers a letter from the Prince to be a matter for his superiors in Rome and in the USA to be informed about. It is a "let's set the record straight" letter.

In his first letter, the Prince meets critique with critique. "Set your own house in order," he says, without reference to the substantive content of Canon Tucker's first letter. His last letter (30 March 1955) is dramatic, subjective, scolding, forgiving, and ends with affectionately yours.

Hurt feelings. Yes, but much more. The insecurity of a lonely Prince shows through.

But he was not too insecure to express his feelings boldly and, at the same time, ask for reassurance. For, at that time in matters of state, his trusted advisors were his father, Prince Pierre and Canon Tucker.

Evidently that reassurance came quickly — personally, not in writing.

It was another short-term "glitch" in a harmonious relationship. Much was stirring in Monaco at that time, and Grace Kelly made her first appearance.

— 8 —
The Promenade - 1954

"Well, my friend, your Prince is still here!"

The Yankee traveler had returned after five years to check on the "cliff hanger" status of the Grimaldis in Monaco and to collect his bet.

"Yes, he has surprised us but we are still very nervous," the Monagasque shopkeeper replied.

"Why? What does he have to do to convince you that he means to rule?"

"In a way, that's the problem. His ambitious plans worry many of us because they will mean great changes here. Our lives will change, our property too valuable to keep, maybe thousands of more residents, and we native Monagasques are already greatly outnumbered."

"Yes, but you are the first-class citizens, the ones who can vote, are you not? You do have control!"

"Less than you think. The Prince has the last say on everything and he's in a continuing battle with the National Council that opposes everything he wants to do!"

"So that's why there is so little change here! The casino is much nicer, but the rest is much the same. Why is the National Council so stubborn?"

"There are several reasons, my friend. For years and years the Council ran things here. Old Prince Louis was only here about 2 months a year. Now the young Prince lives here and is determined to rule here. If he cannot, we think he will leave."

"So there's another threat, but you say there are other reasons!"

"This is more than gossip, my friend. The President of the National Council, Jean Charles Rey, a lawyer, has married Princess Antoinette, the Prince's sister, and claims that she is the rightful heir since she was first born. It won't work, but it is another problem for the Prince, and there are others who claim the throne that are not worth mentioning."

"And what do you think of Onassis?"

"Ah! That is a perceptive question. He has taken over the casino company and is locating much of his business management here. And though the Prince and he are friends, we know their ideas differ about what Monaco can become. Someday there will be a conflict for sure, Mediterranean style. Onassis could win, if we owe him too much!"

"Even the good news is bad news, it seems. Is the Prince still in love with his cars?"

"To the point of death, sir, to the point of death. As you may have heard, he entered a Grand Prix de France under an assumed name and was injured in an accident. Not seriously, thank God. He makes light of it, as is his manner in so many things. And scuba diving! Again, he overextends himself."

"As I remember, in 1949, you were worried about cars, women, and no real need for the job. It seems now that he wants the job, and he wants his cars, but what about women?"

"What about women, indeed? We do not know. Mademoiselle Gisele Pascal, the prince's girlfriend, left for Paris about a year ago. Their 6-year affair has ended for sure and we think she ended it to get on with her acting career."

"And does he have a new girlfriend?"

"No, not like Gisele! He loves women, but he does not seem to be a woman chaser."

"Sounds like he is ready for a princess. Is there a prospect?"

"None! None that we know of, and we are watching. He tells us not to rush him. In a few years and so on. Meanwhile, we have no heir. You know that is our greatest concern."

"I'll bet that he's more ready than you think. He's proven he likes having a woman around. Does he have hobbies that can distract him?"

"Many, and he has a new one. After Gisele left, he decided to start a zoo. He loves animals. And what animals! The bigger and more fierce the better. Lions, a tiger, monkeys and more. He handles them person-ally. The man is fearless!"

"A zoo, another good thing to worry about. He becomes more inter-esting all the time! I wonder if I can get another bet that he will remain as Prince another 5 years. But, tell me, looking back over 5 years, in what ways has Prince Rainier surprised you the most?"

"He is religious, believe it or not, religious. He is becoming more committed to it all the time!"

"Now, that is hard to believe. Tell me more."

"Do you remember that, 5 years ago, I told you this is a Catholic country? Well, one of the first things that Rainier did as Head of State was to visit Pius XII at Rome. During the visit he asked for a change of clergy at San Carlo parish and got it — and things haven't been the same here since."

"Oh, how so?"

"The Vatican sent an American Priest, a Father Francis Tucker, who has really made San Carlo come alive. He wants involvement from everyone, including the Prince, has removed all special privileges, has taught us how to spoil children, American-style, and he has not been bashful about it."

"I will have to visit San Carlo or Saint Charles to check this out. It sounds interesting."

"If you go, take money. He would appreciate it. He considers financial support a sign of faith."

"Put your money where your mouth is, as we say in America. We understand that."

"He is a great preacher — French, Italian, English, and very much into social action. That's what makes him so different."

"Can you explain that? In America our clergy, whether Protestant, Catholic, or Jewish, tend to be socially active."

"He believes we are complacent about living as Catholics. Maybe he is right. For many of us, religion means being baptized — a celebration; confirmed — a celebration; married — a celebration; and buried — a somber celebration — all within the Church. The main process is in education by attending a parochial school. La Pere Tookaire demands that we live as Christians every day. In doing so, he's firm but understanding."

"Well and good, but how about the rest of your clergy?"

"He drives them crazy. Our bishop would have gotten rid of him long ago but could not. Father Tucker was appointed directly by Rome. In fact, the old bishop was retired last year and replaced by Bishop Barthe, who is on good terms with Father Tucker!"

"It figures that Tucker must pay some price for this in this den of iniquity."

"You are right! The press, particularly the French and British press, have tried to ridicule him unmercifully but with no success. He actually seems to enjoy the attention. And then there are the highly placed slander mongers who will invent any lie to destroy an adversary. Unfortunately, there is a type of press that will print anything about a celebrity. One can only live with it, even though embarrassed by it."

"How long can he keep being such a dynamo?"

"Another good question. He is already 65 years old. We, the complacent, expect the Mediterranean effect to slow everyone down. Live and let live. But not La Pere Tookaire, not so far. He is a man with a mission, and he hasn't accomplished it yet."

"Oh! and what is that?"

"To see the Prince make a good marriage. We are sure that is it. That is why we made a mass pilgrimage to Lourdes. That is what we pray for."

"Oh, the Prince again. Father Tucker and he are good friends, I take it."

"Deep friends, indeed. Soon after his arrival, the Prince invited Father Tucker to be the chaplain to the Royal family. The relationship is interesting. Father Tucker looks upon the Prince as a protege, almost as a son. The Prince, in turn, makes it all happen. It is a "destiny" for both of them, and we benefit by it."

"Well, all in all, it seems the Prince is prepared to stay. He needs to get married, to control Onassis, to outsmart the National Council, not to kill himself, and hope that crazy things don't happen in France. I think I'll look for another bet. I'm backing the Prince. Once again, thank you, my friend, perhaps we will meet again."

— 9 —
Mission Accomplished
1955 to 1956

This chapter covers the years 1955–56. In April 1955, Prince Rainier met Grace Kelly for the first time. In December 1955, he proposed marriage and was accepted. In April 1956, Grace Kelly became Princess Grace. In January 1957, Princess Caroline was born.

Father Tucker could, indeed, say mission accomplished. But his mission as pastor of Saint Charles continued.

Since Father Tucker made several trips to the United States during these years, he wrote fewer letters to Joe and Edna. In none of his letters prior to the engagement of Grace and Rainier did he hint at a romance or his support-player role in it. That romance is most accurately recounted in Jeffrey Robinson's *Rainier and Grace* published in the United States by the Atlantic Monthly Press. It reveals that Grace and Rainier became "pen pals" immediately after their first meeting. The more they wrote, the more intimate they became and the more reflective. By the end of October, the Prince was ready to propose but had to be sure he would be accepted. He heard "yes" at the end of December 1955.

And where was the Canon in all of this? Intimately but discreetly involved. It was imperative that the press nor anyone else get wind of this budding romance, and they did not. Thank God, or it might not have happened!

Father Tucker's involvement in the romance and marriage will be the main theme of the following without being a biographically definitive statement.

About Grace

As Father Tucker has said, immediately after Grace's first meeting with Rainier, he wrote to thank her for showing the prince what an American Catholic girl could be. She wrote him a "thank you" note in return. He also told the prince that "Grace is the type of girl I would like to see you marry." And nature took its course.

Jeffrey Robinson reports that some people remain convinced to this day that Father Tucker had used his connections (clerical) in Philadelphia to check out Grace. That he had such connections is true. That he used them is likely, though his family has no direct knowledge that he did. What we do know is that in May 1955 he visited Wilmington, Delaware on Oblate business, at which time he could easily have made inquiries about the Kellys and Grace. He knew of the Kellys but had never met them. In any case, there needed to be an informed mediator between the Grimaldis and Kellys — one who could judge that a true Catholic marriage and not a marriage of convenience was possible. He knew where the Prince stood, but what about Grace? Later, he would be able to give assurances to Grace's parents about the Prince.

The word — the true word — about Grace Kelly is that she had been raised in a Catholic family by a mother who was a convert, had been trained by nuns to know what the religion demanded, and never ceased practicing her religion no matter what the vicissitudes of her life. Doubtless she had experienced the conflicts of "Ryan's Daughter," had her share of the untamed spirit of an Irish soul. But when the chips were down, she made the Christian decision.

Father Tucker would have also found out that there was currently no man in her life, nor scandal. She had caused no divorce, had taken no other woman's husband. (Gossips will say that while that is true, she may have done some short-term borrowing.) She was not exploitive and couldn't stand people who were. She would permit no "cheesecake" exploitation by her studio. She was loyal to her friends, loved children. She was feminine to a level that could drive men to distraction. She did not like conflict and could cry easily. She was poised, gracious, tough, and tenacious. He also realized that, by her choice of careers and success in it, she would need a "theater" for both motherhood and a wifely role. But it would have to be real. She had a passion to be real. I am sure that Father Tucker could conceive of no better choice to be the "real" princess that Monaco would need. A "green light" for the Prince.

About Rainier

Was he ready for a true Catholic marriage? He could not point to one in this century's Grimaldi history. He has provided his own answer in an interview with Jeffrey Robinson.

Obviously, the state religion is Catholicism because the Grimaldis are Catholic, yet Rainier admits to having had many questions over the years about his faith.

He credits Father Tucker with keeping him in the Church.

"I rebelled the way many people do. I had a lot of questions and no one could give me satisfactory answers. But Father Tucker understood my rebellion from the Church and didn't over-dramatize it. That's the way he got me coming back toward the Church. He explained things. He didn't force anything on me the way some other priests probably would have. Let's be honest; most of them, I suspect, would have tried to convince me that by questioning my personal relationship with the Church, I'd committed a great sin. He had an important influence on my life!"

Among other things, he helped Rainier see what the Church should be.

"What is the Church? It's charity, tolerance, and understanding, isn't it? That's also what Father Tucker was all about."

Rainier wanted a real marriage — one based on love, understanding, and shared basic values. He wanted to be real as husband and father. He had thought things through. Both Grace and he became ready at the same time. Even two years previously, they would not have been. They were still getting "their heads on straight." Rainier, too, had a passion to be real. A "green light" for Grace. Somehow, Uncle Francis seemed to know when a head was on straight and when it needed fixing.

A CHRISTMAS GREETING — 1954

To you, my dear Joe and Edna, the best of my wishes!
My thoughts of HOME at Christmas are, of course, of your
HOME, which is the Grand Central of today's TUCKER clan.
All roads seem to lead to it from Rome, Germany, Monte Carlo,
the Far West and points East, not to mention local stations.

It must be some consolation to you to realize the fact, apart the dubious glamour of the Patriarchal Halo such glory bestows.

With every Good Wish for Christmas and the New Year
You have generously shared the honors with me, fashioned by no wilfulness of my own, to be brother, uncle, and granduncle, with new prospects in the offing!
If children are the crown of their parents, and children are counted by generations, you two will be wearing in heaven a tiara one story higher than that of the Pope.

I can't be but grateful that affinity will thus add lustre to my own diadem, but what price glory? The brood should have been taught rhythm at Grandma's knee while she was humming "Silent Night!"

I've played the role of Santa at Trieste. I'll do my best to get to Frankfort. As for Colorado, my God! I blessed your marriage but never to such an extent!

Love and prayers
JFT

Joe and Edna's children were building a family in the 1950's, as were the offspring of brothers Edward and Bill. Family members received no formal training in the rhythm method of birth control, but did learn why it is known disrespectfully as Vatican Roulette.

But, seriously, Father Tucker recognized the importance of maintaining a harmonious relationship between husband and wife in their marriage. On good authority, he is alleged to have told one highly placed woman that it is a worse sin to have her husband "sleep under the bed" than to avoid the conjugal act because of concern about Church strictures on birth control.

*Le Chaplain du Palais
de Son Altesse Serenissime
le Prince de Monaco*

Dear Edna:

*I'll be on the lookout for the Hubers. It's always great to greet
someone from home.*

*Nary a word from Germany, save a card at Xmas from the
Taylors. On the other hand, I didn't write either, not knowing
the addresses. I'm worked to death over here, more than ever
I was at Saint Anthony's. And I have no secretary, could use
three in three languages. Doll sent me a clipping about Joan
Stork, and I sent her the enclosed. My innate modesty and
inherited shyness suffer beyond endurance at this front-page
exposure in the International Press. What I have always loved
about publicity is the way it annoys others; none but the brave
can stand it!*

*I have a bad cold: electric pad, Vicks, nose-drops, aspirin,
and syrup.*

Love to the old-man, and all!

JFT

The International Press seems to have really discovered Canon Tucker
in 1954–1955. A careful review of his ancestors on both the Hickey
and Tucker sides failed to reveal to whom he could attribute his inherited shyness.

Le Chaplain du Palais
de Son Altesse Serenissime
le Prince de Monaco
February 16, 1955

My dear Joe:
I just got your letter of 11th with items of the living and the
dead. The latter seem to be crowding us out, albeit leaving the
fond hope that at the same time they may be swelling the
welcome committee that awaits our tardy arrival. Besides, you
always were late to get to the appointed place. And, as a matter
of fact, I consider this the wisest policy at the approach of dead
end. No sense to be blocked there till plenary indulgence
catches up with you.
... I've been written up in every paper in Europe, and now
the Saturday Evening Post has sent its correspondent to get a
story of me. The impression is that I can wreck or save a
kingdom, while my only concern is to save my own soul and
skin!
Then to think that you would bemoan the fate of losing the
three or four teeth that nature had kindly kept intact for you
against the uninterrupted rough usage you so ruthlessly
submitted their delicate partners-in-crime through what Abe
Lincoln called three score years and ten! If I recall well, Uncle
Joe was cracking walnuts with his teeth on his deathbed!
Which proves how sadly our generation has deteriorated.
Besides, he never used a tooth brush. This may of course be the
reason why his wedlock with Aunt Katie, who wiped her teeth
with a face towel, never did lock.
I'd love to get to see the family in Germany, but think the
chances slim. Never was I busier in my long and colorful
career. I've found time to write a letter to Time and Newsweek
for their February 21 issue, on a subject dear to my heart,

because Dean Pike's positive law would have ruled me out!
Love to Edna. I treated the Hubers well!
JFT

It's quite likely that he was written up in every paper in Europe. He was helping create a new interest in Monaco and change the world view of it with the full support of Prince Rainier. An article titled *A Battling Priest in a Gambling Town* by Paul Hennisort appeared in the December 7, 1955 issue of the *Saturday Evening Post*. He was even beginning to get the attention of Hollywood.

Humorous, irreverent Aunt Katie was everyone's favorite. Family lore has it that she was introduced to Uncle Joe Featherstone, a tobacco salesman, by Monsignor Lyons of Saint Peter's Cathedral in hope that a romance would blossom that would be an antidote to Joe's fondness for spirits. Aunt Katie of all people. Old Joe did shape up some, proving the power of prayer. They became a singing duet in the choir of Saint Peter's and Sacred Heart parishes, possessing a talent based largely on courage.

Le Chaplain du Palais
de Son Altesse Serenissime
le Prince de Monaco
April 3, 1955

Dear Joe and Edna:
It's the evening of Palm Sunday. I said Mass aboard a US Destroyer in port at Monte Carlo at 8:30. Then at the Palace at 10. Presided, as a Canon in robes, at 11 and 12 here at Saint Charles.

Preached, of course, in diverse tongues at these different functions, the gist of my pious meditation being that Christ suffered all this because Judas loved money. And proof that they were all in his class is the fact that the price they put on the Lord is not thirty pieces of silver, but five francs (1-1/2), in the collection.

A Mr. and Mrs. Bedell came to see me this week from Westover Hills, friends of Helen File and Durneys.

I have no news from Germany, and no chance of getting there. Let's hope to meet them all at our "real" Home.

Did you, Joe, have a birthday the 31st of March? I stopped counting mine 6 years ago; my memory sort of went blank. I know that I'm older than Ed, according to his working statistics, which means that you must be all of sixty?

Happy Easter. I'm always praying for Francis, and all of you.

JFT

Mary Hickey Tucker's sons, Joseph and Edward, had a shared talent for not knowing how old they were. This talent was honed by a strong desire not to be forced into retirement because of age. Joseph's reductions were generally in the 4-to-6-year range depending on circumstances. On the date of this letter, he was 71 and still working full-time.

This last letter was written just 3 days before Grace Kelly's meeting with Prince Rainier, during a photo session at the palace in Monaco on April 6, 1955. However, that was not Grace's first visit to the palace surrounds. In the summer of 1954, she was at Nice, France acting in "To Catch a Thief" with Cary Grant. Grace was aware that there was an ancient castle in Monaco, the home of an unmarried prince. One evening, she had a film crew member drive her to "The Rock" so that she could view the castle and its surroundings.

Her curiosity may have been enhanced later by an article appearing in the February 1955 issue of McCall's Magazine. "This Bachelor Prince Needs a Wife" by Morton Sontheimer suggested that the prince hoped to find an American girl to share his throne. Much of the article is based on a personal interview with Prince Rainier, a rare event. One can suspect the fine hand of Canon Tucker in arranging for the interview. Following as it did the Prince's pilgrimage to Lourdes, made in part to affirm a commitment to a Catholic marriage, the article reflects a "reaching out" to someone out there, someone in the United States as publication by McCall's would suggest. The article emphasizes that he is a devout Catholic and a robust man.

More about Lourdes

In a press interview while visiting his nephew, J. Clifton Tucker, in Norwich, Connecticut, July 1960, Father Tucker said "The prince is the same man who said to me on the date of his engagement to Princess Grace on December 29, 1955, 'Father, I owe all of this to you.' I replied to that, no you don't, my Lord Prince. Do you remember our pilgrimage to Lourdes in 1954? Well, there is the 'Grace' the Blessed Mother gave you."

After that, Father Tucker said he related the incident to Princess Grace, who said, "And Father, my confirmation name was Bernadette."

And this brief note by a Father James Gibbons.

"Shortly after Father Tucker arrived in Monte Carlo as chaplain to the Count of Monaco, he persuaded the Prince to go to Lourdes to pray for an ideal future princess. He found her in Princess Grace. Maybe this explains why the Royal Family donated $125,000 to the new underground Chapel of Saint Pius X at Lourdes. Over the Prince's throne is the motto, 'With the Help of God' as we would say 'God Help Us.' The Princess by her devout Catholic life had tremendous influence on the religious life of the people of Monaco."

◆◆◆

Le Chaplain du Palais
de Son Altesse Serenissime
le Prince de Monaco
June 7, 1955

My dear Joe:

*... About my showing up in summer, I don't think so, but I'm
determined to spend Xmas with you, whether the Prince comes
over or not. You never know with these royal birds. As I told
you, I can't afford to go to Germany. One reason, the German
Oblates would expect, as ALL European Oblates do, a
handout. And I haven't got it. My Italian decoration makes my
diplomatic mission at Monaco complete, with the French
Legion of Honor and the local Monaco Knight of Saint
Charles, covering all three Governments whose people I serve.
I'm glad to learn of Ed's retirement, which surely would justify
my own. The Oblates are giving me a raw deal, the dumb
General and the ingrate selfish French leaving me to do a
young man's job, which all of them put together wouldn't and
couldn't do. I'm tired and feel that the willing horse has run
his course. I've done honor to them, as none of them could
have done to themselves over here. And over there, I left them
fat pastures to graze on.*

Cheerio! And lots of love to Ed and all,

The General is still dumb, the French curates are still ingrates, and
our uncle is angry about being overworked. Things seem to be normal.

The following announcement appeared in the *Wilmington Morning
News* on June 3, 1955.

Former City Priest
Honored By Italians

*The rank of Knight of the Order of Merit has been conferred by
the Italian Government on a former Wilmington priest, the
Very Reverend Canon J. Francis Tucker, OSFS, pastor of Saint
Charles' Parish, Monte Carlo, and chaplain to the royal
household of Monaco. Announcement of the latest honor
received by Father Tucker was made here yesterday by the*

Very Reverend William D. Buckley, OSFS, provincial superior of the Oblate Order of Saint Francis de Sales.

Father Buckley said that a cablegram he had received from Rome stated that the knighthood conferred on Father Tucker was in recognition of his work for the people of Italian descent, both in Monte Carlo and in Wilmington. Father Tucker, who established Saint Anthony's Parish more than 30 years ago at the direction of the late Most Reverend Dr. John J. Monaghan, then bishop of Wilmington, served as its pastor for 25 years. He has been in Europe since 1949.

Uncle Francis did not write again until he sent a brief note on August 24, 1955. Orchestrating a further contact between Prince Rainier and Grace Kelly became a private joint venture between priest and Prince. The year 1955 was very difficult for the Prince. It included a financial crisis in Monaco and strained relations with the National Council, though he never wavered in his vision of what he wanted Monaco to become.

It seemed imperative that the Prince must visit the United States if Grace Kelly was to be met again. The Christmas Season seemed to be the best time. The Prince had agreed to attend a charity ball in Manhattan on January 6, 1956 before meeting Grace. It was also decided that the Prince should have a medical checkup at Johns Hopkins, accompanied by a Dr. Donat of Monaco. Canon Tucker, in turn, was scheduled to celebrate on January 8, 1956 at Saint Anthony's Church, Wilmington, Delaware the 50th anniversary of his religious profession in the Order of Oblates of Saint Frances de Sales. All three of these proposed events occurred. They were not subterfuges.

But how were prince and actress to meet? One way was by a request for the Prince to visit her at work in the shooting of the movie "The Swan." Another was for Divine Providence to take a hand, though the Austins may say they did it all on their own. Close enough to the Kellys to be called Aunt and Uncle, on a visit to Monaco the Austins met Prince Rainier and Canon Tucker, had tea with them, talked about the Kellys, and invited the Prince to visit them "if and when." "If and when" became Christmas day, the Austins arranging for priest, prince, and doctor to visit the Kellys. Father Tucker made many of the arrangements, but the prince, by way of Jeffrey Robinson, now tells that Grace and he had decided to meet sometime during his own 2-month visit. There were no leaks.

Post Card — August 24, 1955

Dear Joe,
I'm making my retreat here alone with the good Swiss
Benedictine monks. It's great, and I love it, much as I needed it
both physically and spiritually. I'm praying for you and Edna.
Keep well and happy with all yours.
        JFT

Uncle Francis did love the 10-day period of this annual retreat. He could rest, relax, "get his own head on straight," the best kind of vacation to support a vocation. His next 12 months would be eventful beyond expectation.

Le Chaplain du Palais
de Son Altesse Serenissime
le Prince de Monaco
September 4, 1955

My dear Joe:
... I want to get home to see you and to be seen. The latest news
on this phase is: sailing aboard the United States from Havre
November 24th, with the Prince and his doctor and secretary.
Medical check-up for the Prince at Johns Hopkins early De-
cember, when I'll get home to you. The rest of the program is
uncertain. I hope to spend Xmas with you, with exemption from
the role of Santa Claus for the 32 representatives of the 3rd
generation. Yes! I'm paying my own way. You'll understand
why. What price independence! Bill Raskob wrote that he will

help. Meanwhile, thanks for your own good constant lifts. So glad the gang's all there! Would rather meet them at HOME than anywhere else in this tired part of the world.

Love to Edna and all — and cheerio till we meet in the USA!

As ever,
JFT

No mention of a romance here or of a firm "program," other than a medical check-up, but the arranging of a program was "in the works."

Once again, Uncle Francis maintained his financial independence from the royal household. He was not to be a "broker" of any kind. Once again, his support would come from staunch friends in Delaware, Bill Raskob, among them. He had his own justification for a trip, his 50th year celebration of his religious profession, to be held on his 67th birthday.

One program requirement was to inform the American public, and in particular, the Kellys, about what kind of a man the Prince of Monaco was and of his aspiration for finding the right woman. The solution was an article based on a personal interview with the Prince titled "His Kingdom for a Bride" by David Schoenbrun that was published in *Collier's Magazine* in the late Fall of 1955. Aside from its insights about the character of the Prince himself, it clearly indicated that the kind of woman the Prince did *not* care for Grace Kelly *wasn't* and the kind of woman he sought, she *was*. And *he* was the kind of gallant, sensitive, sophisticated man Grace liked and the kind of skilled, daring "macho" man the Kellys liked. A fine article, difficult to improve on.

Evidently, the Prince thought so. He gave the interview with the proviso that he be permitted to read, edit, and approve a pre-publication draft of the article. That approval was given October 20, 1955 with only a few minor editorial suggestions.

Though Schoenbrun's article, it may have been Canon Tucker's idea.

Le Chaplain du Palais
de Son Altesse Serenissime
le Prince de Monaco
November 11, 1955

My dear Joe:
... The Prince had to delay his departure owing to unfortunate foolish political manoeuvrings by some of his loyal subjects. I delayed mine for his sake. I think he will be in Wilmington for my birthday, January 8th. I shall be there earlier. As I see it now, I shall have to stay with him in N.Y. over the 18th to assist at Mass at Saint Patrick's. Then he will come to Johns Hopkins, and I'll go there with him, but shall commute to Wilmington during his stay. He is going to Havana for Xmas, but I shall be with you. He must be in N.Y. for January 6th to preside at a big gala event. I'll meet him there and then come with him to Wilmington, Saturday, 7th. We'll be at Saint Anthony's the 8th, he will stay a couple of days at Hotel Du Pont and go from there to Atlantic City, Philadelphia, etc. and then start West. All this is subject to change by the State Department, but I'll be with you as long and as often as I can. His visit is to last two months.

Tell Edna and Phyl that I think of them each day at Mass, often in my dreams.

Love to all,
JFT

Father Tucker's nephew, Cliff, an Army Officer, underwent surgery for removal of a large non-malignant growth in his chest at an Army hospital in Denver about this time. His recovery was complete.

There is no mention of Grace Kelly in this letter. The events on December 16, January 6, and January 8, were firm. Evidently, the prince was to find opportunities to meet Grace Kelly after January 8th. Having decided to ask her to marry him, he wanted to be reasonably certain that she would accept.

It is likely that the Christmas day visit with the Kellys by way of the Austins had not been arranged because it was not certain that Grace would have completed her work on "The Swan." When it became certain that she could be home by Christmas day, the program was complete. The Prince forgot about Havana.

Rainier and Grace became engaged on December 29, 1955 but held the formal announcement until January 6, 1956.

Father Tucker had several crucial liaison tasks. Before sailing, he visited the Prince's mother, Princess Charlotte, at her estate at Marchais, France to inform her of her son's intentions. She said only that she hoped her son would marry a good Catholic girl.

Later, Father Tucker informed John Kelly of the Prince's desire to marry Grace. The discussion included reassuring information about the Prince's financial state. Kelly was persuaded. The Kellys were delighted for Grace.

The following is an article from *The Journal — Every Evening*, Wilmington, Delaware, January 6, 1956.

Father Tucker Joins Prince, Fiancée in Big Charity Ball

(Royal Chaplain of Rainier III and Miss Kelly To Attend "Night in Monte Carlo" Affair; Cleric To Celebrate Anniversary Here Sunday)

———————————

A solemn religious anniversary will have priority on the busy week-end schedule of Prince Rainier III of Monaco and his royal chaplain, the Wilmington-born Very Reverend Dr. J. Francis Tucker.

The priest, for 25 years pastor of Saint Anthony's Catholic Church here, will join the prince and his fiancee, actress Grace Kelly, in New York City tonight for a huge "Night in Monte

Carlo" charity ball at which Father Tucker will represent the prince's family.

Then the 32-year-old monarch and his chaplain will return to Wilmington to prepare for 11:15 a.m. solemn high mass on Sunday, which Father Tucker will celebrate to mark the 50th anniversary of his religious profession in the order of Oblates of Saint Francis de Sales. They will be dinner guests of Mr. and Mrs. W.F. Raskob tomorrow night.

Coincidentally, Sunday will also be the jubilarian's 67th birthday.

Father Tucker spent today in Wilmington attending to business details at the royal suite in the Hotel Du Pont.

Members of Saint Anthony's parish, friends of the priest, and clergy from a number of communities are expected to fill Saint Anthony's Church for the mass.

An invitation luncheon will follow in Fournier Memorial Hall on Howland Street, at which the Very Reverend William D. Buckley, American provincial of the Oblates, will be toast-master. Father Buckley will also preach the sermon at the mass.

Sunday's religious and social occasions are postponed American celebrations of Father Tucker's entry into the Oblates, not of his ordination as a priest, which followed his profession by several years. The anniversary actually was last October.

If the Prince and his Monacoan companions had any doubt about Father Tucker's moral and political clout in Delaware, the "gala" in Wilmington on January 8th would have dispelled them. The Solemn High Mass at Saint Anthony's Church was attended by hundreds, with many distinguished guests including Prince Rainier; Grace's parents, Mr. and Mrs. John Kelly; Mr. Marcel Palmero, Consul General of Monaco and his wife; August F. Walz, Mayor of Wilmington; close family members; and many clergy.

There were many highlights at the testimonial dinner. A cable Apostolic Blessing from Pius XII, a telegram of good wishes from Grace Kelly who was on her way back to Los Angeles, the conferring of "honorary" Delaware citizenship upon Prince Rainier, the presentation of the "key" to the city of Wilmington to the Prince by Major August F. Walz, and, to the Governor's complete surprise, the conferring of the Order of Merit of the Knighthood of Saint Charles upon Governor Boggs by Prince Rainier. The guests included Harris B. McDowell, the U.S. Representative from Delaware, and Mr. John Pochna, international lawyer of Monaco and his wife. It was a grand affair with speeches, tributes and responses galore. And Uncle Francis received a "purse" in four figures which he badly needed. The next day he got back to business, for a "cloud of uncertainty" had arisen.

"Prince leaves for Florida with Nuptial Plans Cloudy" said the *Wilmington Morning News* of January 10, 1956. Paul Noches, chief of the prince's private Cabinet, had announced the wedding would be in Monaco. That was news to the Kellys, for that wasn't the American way. An irritated Canon fired this blast to the Prince.

Oblates of Saint Francis De Sales

OFFICE OF THE PROVINCIAL
2100 BANCROFT PARKWAY
WILMINGTON 6, DELAWARE
AMERICAN PROVINCE

My dear Lord Prince:
May I submit to Your good consideration what I have
understood of my position in the matter of Your engagement:
Since first I knew of Your attitude towards Grace, I took it
upon myself to serve as liaison between You and the Kellys.
From the first and all through my endeavor, my policy was to
write and speak and act as I gathered You wanted from our
conversations, employing such tact as is my command to
safe-guard the intimate and delicate implications in the case. I
was inspired and encouraged in this by Your own very tactful
and superb handling of persons and matters involved. To the

115

great delight of the American people, You sold Yourself to them as a Man rather than as a Prince, without detracting from but rather adding to the dignity and worth of Your Sovereignty.

So when this clamor broke about the place of the wedding and that, on the one hand, Noches issued an edict that it would take place over there, and that, on the other hand, Mrs. Kelly, when asked, said she knew nothing about it, it was clear to me that You could not be presented as subject to Your own Government and much less as discourteous to the family of the bride.

Mr. Kelly is terribly obligated to the people of Philadelphia. Out of two million, all but 65 thousand voted for him to be their mayor. While he is not obligated to them as You are to Your people by a title far superior, it is easy to understand that he cannot change overnight their mentality or the American tradition that the marriage belongs to the place of the bride. This is the FIRST time in modern history that an American girl marries a Prince. And while all are agreed to respect the differences this match brings with it, these differences cannot be imposed in a dictatorial way such as Noches' maladroit communication implied.

Now comes Palmaro's statement, published in all the news, about financial arrangements: "It takes weeks and months to settle such matters because this is not a question of any Tom, Dick or Joe (we generally say Harry), and that all this MUST be decided by the PALACE." This is really awkward, because it still, just like the Noches announcement, puts You under the Palace, and makes the American public ask if Grace is marrying the Monaco Government or You. You must get this point of view, my dear Lord Prince: You are right in not wanting to be "Mr. Grace Kelly," but then Grace wants to be Your Wife and Your Princess and not "Mrs. Monaco" subject not to You, nor to Noches, Palmaro and Co. There she is "any Maggie, Sally, or Lucille." I think that these guys are seeking their own importance, above all, and that they resent particularly my "interference" as I *mentioned to You over the phone.*

Please understand that the Kellys LOVE You very, very much and they respect You. Mrs. Kelly always refers to You as His Highness and so does John in public life. They will give You their all, but in their own way. They are giving You the BEST they have, and all America thinks that they too are giving You their BEST. And they give her willingly to You, thanking God that it is You.

But don't let these simpletons step in, with their fifteenth century ideas which I know You loathe, to spoil the magnificent job You have done WITHOUT them.

The Kellys now WANT the wedding in Monaco, but John B. cannot assume the responsibility of the decision as coming from the family of the bride, nor can he very well make it appear that the Monaco Government's decision was imposed on him.

He would like me, an American, Your friend and theirs, to say that while the Prince has been most deferent to their desires, it would seem to Europeans that a slight was being made to Grace if she were not accorded all the royal honors at the wedding that Your position calls for that a bride of royal lineage would be accorded. The Monagasque people want HER to have these honors.

With such a presentation of the case, John will be "taken off the hook," as he says, and the people of America will understand.

Remember, this is the FIRST case of this kind in our American History — the case of Prince Albert never struck the American imagination as this one does, because America thinks Grace is their property.

About the time.

I know that You come over things I have said in the past, as with my first ideas that coincided with Yours on the place. New reactions from the public both in Monaco and here bring changes.

Taking a house in California and waiting around until Grace finished her work would give the press a lot of wild criticism, and Grace's hard schedule would leave You little time with her.

It would be dignified if You took her mother to see Your mother, and showed her Le Palais and Iberia, while Grace is working. Nothing can tie You and Grace more tightly than that same Mother and both Mothers, and that will set well with the public.

Then let John B. come over to bring her home. If there's an interval between pictures, that is, if the second is to be done, why can't You come over too?

Getting married, my Lord Prince, even with ordinary people is not a simple affair. I've often heard young men say that if they knew all this bother attached to it, they would have become Oblates. But it is WORTH all this bother, and delay and fuss.

Grace is YOURS, my Lord Prince, and this is the ONLY thing that matters. What more do these Monagasques want?

I got a beautiful letter from Bishop Barthe: He tells me he was in Rome with Gahlan at the Grand Hotel when the news broke over the radio. I had written him about it.

"Le Cardinal Spellman etait la, et m'a dit sa joir d'apprendre ce CHOIX du Prince." At the Hotel, the director brought out a photo showing John B. Kelly with the Cardinal at the time he got the red hat. At Saint Suzannes (Not malard), where the Bishop was saying mass, the American priests "etaient tout heureuz de chanter les louanges de Mademoiselle Grace. Au retour j'ai trouve la Principaute en liesse."

Pour moi, je me rejouis a la pensee que notre Prince va pouvoir donner libre cours a ses penchants naturels our une vie calme, honnete de bon catholique."

Then he tells me not to mind the nasty cracks taken against me by Noches' silly statement, which put me in the light that I was trying to run the show and usurp the government's role.

After all that those Monagasques said to me about getting You married, now they want to throw a monkey-wrench in the wheels, just because an American in America is trying to help You to run the car — as a back-seat driver, and that's all.

It went all over the U.S. Press, making me look like a cheap publicity seeker, and I think that from what You have seen of me in my country, I don't need to seek it. If those bastards keep that up, I'll not go back to them. I'll have a chapel at Iberia, and let them all go to Siberia.

Put the muzzle on Palmaro and tell him he is a helluva diplomat.

Every mention about Your chaplain in the U.S. Press is that he is a jovial, shrewd, cagey gentleman. I'm just saying this to compare me with Mr. Lucille!

I'm now with the approval of the Archbishop of Philadelphia who saw the script releasing a series of articles on You, as I know You — all meant to let the American Public at large share my esteem and affection for You.

Now please understand me and all that I have written. And don't forget that You are in LOVE, and so mentally unbalanced. You are meeting the biggest challenge a man ever met. All good people want to see it succeed, and it will, with all the good prayers of these Dames de S. Maur, plus the millions that are offered for You in the good old USA, of which You are a citizen of the greatest State in the Union. Cheerio, Mr. Delaware.

Whew! Don't mess with the Irish! The Prince straightened out the announcement issue as suggested. He did not give up on his intent to go to California to be with Grace. He went, and his Chaplain became Chaperon, no doubt, very pleased that the wedding would be in April

119

and the Prince would have to return to Monaco early in March to prepare for it.

The *Philadelphia Inquirer* did publish a 4-series article titled "Prince Rainier As I Know Him" by J. Francis Tucker, OSFS.

Meanwhile, Governor Boggs, of Delaware, sent these two gracious notes to Prince Rainier and Father Tucker.

STATE OF DELAWARE
EXECUTIVE DEPARTMENT
DOVER

J. CALEB BOGGS
GOVERNOR
January 20, 1956

The Very Reverend Doctor J. Francis Tucker
2200 Kentmere Parkway
Wilmington, Delaware

My dear Father Tucker:
The Boggs family and especially our little daughter, Marilyn, are most grateful to you and His Serene Highness, the Prince of Monaco, for his wonderful autographed picture and the most generous note on the card accompanying the picture. You can be sure that Marilyn and all of us prize it highly. You were wonderful to think of this and do little things like this with all of your other important duties. It is things like this, I am sure, that make you the fine, great, and wonderful man and Priest which you are.

Thank you again and please give our very highest respects to His Highness and with all best wishes and highest regards to you, I am
Sincerely yours,
J. Caleb Boggs

✦✦✦

STATE OF DELAWARE
EXECUTIVE DEPARTMENT
DOVER

J. CALEB BOGGS
GOVERNOR
January 12, 1956

His Serene Highness Rainier III
Prince Sovereign of Monaco

Your Highness:
Mrs. Boggs and I wish to express again on behalf of the people of the State of Delaware and ourselves sincere appreciation for the friendship and honor you have extended to us by your visit with us and by your interest and friendship in our community.

May I also thank you both personally and on behalf of the State of Delaware for the honor you so graciously bestowed upon us in presenting me with the Monaco Order of Merit of the Knighthood of Saint Charles. We shall always cherish it with appreciative memories of a very charming and wonderful gentleman, Prince Rainier of Monaco.

We hope that there will be many other occasions when you may have the opportunity to visit us, and we shall look forward with pleasure always to doing all we can to be of service to you, Father Tucker and to your people.

We especially extend to you and your Princess-to-be best wishes for good health, happiness and success in all that you may do.

> *Sincerely yours,*
> *J. Caleb Boggs*
> *Governor*

The January 17, 1956 issue of Wilmington's *The Journal — Every Evening* had this article.

Father Tucker Gets Film Bid
(Neither Producer Nor Priest Will Confirm
Reports of Contract)

A *motion picture contract has been offered the Very Reverend Dr. J. Francis Tucker, chaplain to the royal family of Monaco.*

It was learned today negotiations were started by Leo McCarey, independent Hollywood producer of such films as "Going My Way," with the priest when Father Tucker was in Wilmington and New York City last month.

It is not known whether the offer is for rights to the priest's life story, or whether it also includes any personal services. The latter is doubtful, since Father Tucker is expected to return to his duties in Monaco within three months.

Father Tucker would neither confirm nor deny the report when questioned here. He left yesterday for Florida, apparently to meet Prince Rainier III, ruler of Monaco, who is vacationing there.

Will Go to California

The pair then expects to travel through the Southwest and eventually reach California, where McCarey said negotiations would be resumed.

In a telephone conversation from Wilmington with McCarey in Hollywood yesterday, the producer said he had no comment at present; that negotiations would be resumed when Father Tucker reaches California; and that "there has been no meeting of minds on the matter."

McCarey also said "I promised Father Tucker that if and when an agreement is reached, the publicity would come from him."

No Personal Gain

It is understood that any contract would bring no financial gain to Father Tucker but would, instead, benefit his religious

*order, the Oblates of Saint Francis de Sales, which operates
Salesianum School for Boys. Under the rules of the order, the
Oblates take a vow of personal poverty in addition to other
sacrifices.*

*McCarey, whose hit films have frequently had religious
themes, also produced "The Bells of Saint Mary's."*

Prince Rainier rented a villa in Bel Air for his stay in Los Angeles.
Grace was acting in what would be her last picture, "High Society."
The "Film Bid" was not just a rumor. There were negotiations.

Marymount School
10643 Sunset Boulevard
Los Angeles 24, California
February 21, 1956

My dear Joe:
*It's been little of homecoming for me this trip with all that
chaperoning two royal wooers implies. To add to my worries,
POP Prince Pierre flew in here to father-in-law Grace, after
all he did to balk the romance. I got out of the Princely
Headquarters when he arrived, and took refuge here with the
holy nuns, quite a change from being at receptions, dinners
and teas with Mrs. Gary Cooper, Jack Warner, Rosalind
Russell, Jane Wyman, Bing Crosby, the Cornelius Vanderbilt
Whitneys, Merwin Leroy, and Zsa Zsa Gabor!*

*I have my fifth sitting with Leo McCreary today. Have also
met the Cardinal, the Bishop and a fine lot of clergy. I so
wanted to stop at Denver, but it's out. I can't. I'll be East
around the 27th, and shall contact you. Sailing the 16th.*

*LOVE to Edna and all. Let them have news of me, Eleanor,
and so on.*
As ever,
JFT

Whatever reservations Prince Pierre had regarding the royal romance ended when he met Grace. He was very supportive of her as Princess of Monaco. For her, he was family. They were friends.

Uncle Francis seems to have had a helluva time as chaperon. Evidently, the proposal for a movie about Father Tucker "died on the vine." A likely reason is that it was appropriate for the "spotlight" to turn from Priest to Princess. We do know that he had discussions with executives in Hollywood as late as 1961.

He did sail on March 16th, possibly with the Prince and Count Pierre. They all returned for what was to have been a solemn ceremony and celebration for all in Monaco, only to have a horde of the world press and pseudo-press (TV) attempt with much success to trivialize it by treating it only as theatrical entertainment. The Royal Couple survived it, but as Princess Caroline recounts, were reluctant to talk about it for several years. The Catholic wedding occurred on April 19, 1956.

April 28, 1956
MONACO

Not one leisurely moment has been left to me to write since my return, for obvious reasons. I have been in the middle of all this, both from the Kellys' and from the Grimaldis' side. The opinion of Rome is that I did a good job. So what else matters?

The press has been rotten, partly because out of 1800 newsmen and newswomen only a few could be favored because of space, and the rest vented their spleen against the Prince, the Kellys and the Tuckers.

I have received over 5,000 letters from all the continents, one out of twenty against.

Dorothy Kilgallen gave me a blast. She apologized to the Prince for her article on Marilyn Monroe, and thus got me to get her invited to the affair. And once there, she wrote that rot about me, not a word of it was true, but good reading for her type of minds.

I am going to Rome tomorrow, I am not leaving Grace or the Prince.

This note probably was included in a packet of news items sent by Father Tucker to his brother Joe.

The world must have been thirsting for news for 1800 newspersons to show up for this wedding. They arrived too early, experienced a period of bad weather, had to scramble for housing, and had no one to talk to except themselves. That the Press could have been handled better is a likely conjecture. That an out-of-control Press caused its own problems is a fact.

Dorothy Kilgallen did hit bottom in her "blast" about Father Tucker. Her article that Gisele Pascal was nearby implied that Grace Kelly was second fiddle, was incredibly bad taste, and not true, since Miss Pascal had left two years previously. But the part of her article that infuriated the friends and supporters of Father Tucker was the following:

"Father Tucker is indeed a most unusual clergyman. In manner he is very like a breezy press agent who has somehow acquired permission to say Mass in addition to promoting his client.

He is not reluctant to admit that, but for the grace of God and his own persistence, Prince Rainier might still be dallying amorously with Mlle. Pascal, the populations would be restless, and there would be no happy prospect of an heir to the throne of Monaco."

At least one newspaper included under Dorothy Kilgallen's column this letter to her from the Reverend Edmond P. McCarthy, OSFS.

Father McCarthy Replies to Miss Kilgallen

My dear Miss Kilgallen:
In your column of April 19, you have once again, in your own vitriolic way, set yourself up as judge and jury to annihilate the character of a fellow human being. Indicative of a small mind, the entire column is based on wild and scandalous rumor. This means nothing to you, as your sophomoric comments in the

125

past have proven that you like to "play God." It might be refreshing to your lilliputian mind to give serious thought to the following statements based upon facts and the truth.

To those of us who really know Father Tucker and have come under his priestly and fatherly influence through the years, we heartily agree with this one sentence in your column, "Father Tucker is indeed a most unusual clergyman."

YES, TO THE more than 75,000 boys who have been educated in schools of the Oblates of Saint Francis de Sales in this country, of which Father Tucker was the first American Provincial and founder of most of these schools, to these he "is indeed a most unusual clergyman."

Yes, to the thousands of Italian people in Wilmington, Del., where Father Tucker founded Saint Anthony's Parish and remained for 25 years looking after their spiritual and material welfare, to these people their first shepherd was and remains "a most unusual clergyman."

Yes, to his brother Oblates of the American Province, over whom he ruled for 18 years, to the thousands of priests who, like myself, owe their vocation, after the grace of God, to his inspiration and wise counsel, he "is indeed a most unusual clergyman."

Yes, to the innumerable diocesan priests who have been spiritually strengthened by the words of his sacred eloquence as he preached their annual retreats, to these, too, he "is indeed a most unusual clergyman."

YES, TO THE people of Monte Carlo, where for more than five years as pastor of Saint Charles he had brought about a complete spiritual rejuvenation and untold good, to these also, he "is indeed a most unusual clergyman."

Yes, in his 45 years as a priest, a teacher, as director of souls, as shepherd of this flock, to the rich, the poor, to the learned and unlettered, to saint and sinner, Father Tucker has

126

been "indeed a most unusual clergyman." May God spare him
for many more years that he may continue to be so.

Every task assigned to Father Tucker in his long, fruitful,
and brilliant career has come to him through obedience, which
to him means God's will. Would that everyone (even mothers-
turned-columnist) could say that they are doing God's will, so
that one day we might say of them that which we proudly say of
Father Tucker today, "He has done all things well."

Sincerely yours,
(Rev.) Edmond P. McCarthy, OSFS

Father Tucker never seemed to be deeply upset about press attacks
and held no grudges. In fact, he was well disposed toward a number of
responsible journalists, Art Buchwald being one of them.

Le Chaplain du Palais
de Son Altesse Serenissime
le Prince de Monaco
ROME
May 8, 1956

My dear Joe:
I am to leave Paris by TWA on Flight 831, June 7th to arrive
N.Y. on the 8th at 7:00 A.M.

For the Consecration of Bishop Schlotterback, of course.
But then, also, to see more of you and mine than my last trip
permitted.

That trip was full of events that outguessed even me, and
brought me world-wide renown.

Here in Rome, the bosses are satisfied, and congratulating
me, which means all.

The Press had to have its innings, that's how they make
their living. But, thank God, I weathered the storm. Thanks for
all the news-items, duly received.

You should see the ones from the world press of every country, each picking photos to suit their different tastes.

I'll tell you of all this, face to face. I'm busy, as usual, and more so here in Rome, where everybody now wants me, even the American College.

Hope all are well. Love to Edna, and to all, ever yours,
JFT

Uncle Francis was probably "outguessed" by the rapidity of events concerning the engagement and wedding of Rainier and Grace. She was scheduled to make two pictures for MGM — the latter after the wedding. Legal problems involving the second movie were averted by her becoming pregnant on her honeymoon and a second child followed soon after the first. Goodbye, MGM.

OBLATES DE S-FRANCOIS DE SALES
8 AVENUE SAINT-CHARLES
MONTE-CARLO

MONTE-CARLO, LE
September 8, 1956

My dear Joe:
Your delightful letter was a refresher, evidently a breath of Budweiser visit at Saint Louis. I take it for granted that Edna went to the Cathedral while you paid homage and sought sanctuary in the Brewery, and that both thought of your hapless brother as you fingered your respective beads. My two children, Rainier and Grace, have left for USA, so I am a bit freer though still overbusy. Bill Jeandell will tell you about my life here. He is a grand fellow, the best cousin we have had, on the paternal side of the family. While overseeing the sending of thousands of letters of acknowledgement for the Princess, I have had to let personal correspondence suffer, as much as I

love to write. Very happy to send Sister Florentine and the Missionaries of the Sacred Heart official greeting from Their Highnesses, as also to our Grand-children, now that I know where they are.

Father La Penta is a God-send to me, just the man I need. He is making a great hit with everybody: Bishop, Prince, and people, and even the French Oblates.

I've been on the job full schedule at Saint Charles and Palace for two solid months without a break. I'm getting a change of French curates, thank God, and would rather do all the work alone than continue with the ones I've had.

Love to Ed — As always
JFT

Prince and Princess came to the USA to visit her parents and rejuvenate her spirit. Princess Grace closed out her New York apartment and had much of her furniture sent to the Palace. Father Tucker's responsibility for the Princess' correspondence was to ensure that it was diplomatically correct.

Father Tucker did stay close to Grace and Rainier. John B. Kelly specifically asked him to do so. Kelly knew the first few years would be difficult for Grace.

French curates again! Shaped from the same cookie cutter.

OBLATES DE S-FRANCOIS DE SALES
8 AVENUE SAINT-CHARLES
MONTE-CARLO

MONTE-CARLO, LE
22 October 1956

My dear Joe:
I got your news clippings and the always gratefully received and useful bank notes. I guess you missed an item spread over

the North American Newspaper Alliance about "Rainier's Chaplain on Way Out!" Mrs. La Penta sent a copy to Father Charlie from a Buffalo Paper. I sort of wish it were true. I almost made the new Bishop's Consecration day after tomorrow (24th), had a berth on the United States and all that, but had to cancel owing to an unpredictable emergency requiring my presence here. I had Father General's permission and the Prince's expressed wish that I join Him and Her in USA before their return, but something more important to them and me and all concerned popped up. Having known and served all four Bishops of Wilmington, I would have liked to have done homage to the fifth. I remember Bishop Becker coming to visit Brennans; twas at one of these visits that I served his mass at Saint Peter's. Of course, we often served Bishop Curtis, and were at Bishop Monghan's Consecration as at that of his successor. All this makes interesting history. I learn that the local brethren are disappointed that Monsignor Sweeney did not get it. I am sure that he does not share their feelings: no wise man would.

I'm waiting for Father Lawless and sisters to drop in on me. That's just about what they will do without advance warning. I wouldn't want to be absent when they come. Every cloud has a silver if not golden lining. Then one must always see human events in the light of God's fatherly providential care of us.

More later; I'm terribly Busy. Love to Ed and all,
JFT

We do not know what the emergency was that Father Tucker refers to. Obviously, the Prince depended upon him greatly to assist in crisis management.

Le Chaplain du Palais
de Son Altesse Serenissime
le Prince de Monaco

December 10, 1956

My dear Joe:
Thanks for your letter of November 28th. ... I had my Thanks-
giving dinner alone with "My Two" as the Prince calls himself
and Grace. No turkey, though, a capon! Both seem to cuddle
up to me more than ever, which pleases me a lot. I'm seeing for
myself what the gentry over here say: "They need me." Which
shows again how wrong newsmen can get. I'm working a tough
schedule with the parish taking most of my time because of the
type of help my French confreres give me. They're a sloppy
gang. Thank God Charlie La Penta is a great and good USA
Oblate.
　　I'll have midnight Mass at the Palace and the other two in
the parish and dinner with the Prince and Princess. For the
first time in endless years have piped down on sending cards:
no time! and presents: no money! I live with it all around me,
but that's as far as it gets. MERRY XMAS to all and lots of
LOVE.
　　JFT

Uncle Francis mentions having both Thanksgiving and Christmas
dinner with Grace and Rainier. Mrs. Kelly must have arrived shortly
after Christmas to be with Grace during the final stage of her preg-
nancy.

As usual, Uncle Francis was broke and over busy, unable to get his
French curates off their asses and/or knees.

There is no doubt that Rainier and Grace needed him. The first 2-1/2
years of Grace's marriage were very difficult. In that time she had two
children, learned to speak French like a good American, somewhat
tamed a spirited husband, figured out how to assert herself as both wife
and princess, and had won the affection of the Monacoans.

But, at the beginning, she found that her hard-earned Grace Kelly
identity was gone, and she had no other. She was ill from both morning
sickness and homesickness. The Palace was cold and impersonal, not

home-like. She had no friends nearby, had a language problem, had to learn to manage a household staff, to conform to Palace protocol, tolerate a climate that was not her personal favorite, and had a husband who adored her but had not yet learned how to relate to her with sensitivity.

Were they of different temperaments?

Grace Kelly once said that if she were not an actress, she would like to be a kindergarten teacher. Rainier Grimaldi once said that if he were not the Prince of Monaco, he would like to be a lion tamer. She was a true Scorpio; he, a true Gemini. Grace hated to fight; he loved it. Both hated to lose. He would go for a kill early; Grace would wait until the fight was over, then win it.

Early on, they needed a mediator, a wise and trusted friend, one who they could love and respect. Canon Tucker was that person. In a sense, he was their Uncle Francis, too. He loved it.

OBLATES DE S-FRANCOIS DE SALES
8 AVENUE SAINT-CHARLES
MONTE-CARLO

MONTE-CARLO, LE
10 January, 1957

Dear Mr. and Mrs. Tucker,
Please forgive me for being so tardy in answering your very kind Christmas greetings and accompanying gift. I want to thank you sincerely for your kind and generous remembrance of me at Christmas. Being so far away from home and friends for the first time naturally brought with it a little homesickness, but knowing that it is God's will for me to be here, I am happy, especially since I have such a wonderful superior to work for. I like the work very much — and there's plenty of it. My main duties consist in taking care of the large number of American Catholic families living along the coast of the Riviera, teaching Catechism to their children, hearing confessions, and saying Mass aboard the U.S. Salem when it is in port. And when it is

not in port, I say the 12 o'clock Mass here at the parish, and preach in English. Other duties consist of acting as Father Tucker's secretary and driver, teaching Catechism to the nieces and nephew of the Prince, and, recently, hearing confessions in French.

The weather here is not exactly like Florida's, but, then again, it is not too cold. During the day it is fairly warm, but in the evening a blanket or two is required. Since I have been here, however, we have had rain only four or five times. The food is much the same as in the States, but the people here take their time to eat it. All stores are closed from 12 noon until 2:30 so that families can eat together and leisurely enjoy their meal and, perhaps, even get in a little siesta.

At present the people here are anxiously awaiting the arrival of an heir. The Princess is very much loved by all the people, and always gets a big ovation whenever she appears in public. Several times she has made the citizens of Monaco extremely happy by visiting their stores and making a few purchases. They can be extremely grateful to Father Tucker for his part in bringing this talented, devout and Catholic young woman to Monaco.

On Thursday evening, the 3rd of January, since Father Tucker, Father James Reese and myself were the only priests here, we decided to anticipate Father's birthday American style. We had a grand time and enjoyed ourselves very much. On the actual day of his birthday, the entire community — four of us — were together and we celebrated the occasion with a grand meal at noon. Although Father looks well, he's very tired and, at present, he has a touch of the grippe. When in the States, I often wondered why he rarely answered our letters. Now I know. It's incredible the amount of work and time that is demanded of him. I pray daily that Our Lord will give him the necessary health to continue his good work.

*Well, dear friends, I must sign off for now. Thanks once
again for your kindness, and may the good Lord bless you
always!*

    Sincerely
    Father Charles

Father La Penta was born and raised in Saint Anthony of Padua parish, Wilmington, Delaware. He is one of Father Tucker's "boys." The
nieces and nephews of the Prince he refers to are the children of Princess Antoinette, at that time aged about 11, 9, and 7.

The birthday celebration was Father Tucker's 68th. Father La Penta's
letter gives a perceptive glimpse of an American priest's life at the
Riviera.

Palais de Monaco
January 18, 1957

My dear Joe:
*I got all you sent me, Xmas and Birthday generous greetings
from you and Edna, with contents and your revealing letter,
which unmasks the inner man in question.*

    *One of our boys from Fribourg let me know how
embarrassed the Oblate Community there is over unpaid bill
due the Nuns from whom religious articles including a censer
were bought during his European tour by your man. Letters
have been sent even to the Provincial about this, and the Nuns
are still unpaid and the OSFS discredited. I spent much on my
guests during that tour and obtained substantial gifts for them.
Elaborate promises were made that I would be reimbursed. Not
even a Xmas card came to me. As Uncle Joe Featherstone said:
"You can't trust pin-toed or bow-legged men." True, Uncle
was stingy, but never cheated except for the glory of God.*

    *In the Oblate game of life, a lot of unfairness exists due to a
disregard for the Rule, and this stems from the Mother-house*

down. Of course, such was the Life of Christ under the men in power who would have no power unless it was given them from above. The bargain is that we see God in our superiors "whether good or BAD" and so await the resurrection. I hope you get out nobly.

Right now, I'm pacing the floor waiting for a baby. Am very much in the inner picture but keeping out of the public eye for obvious reasons.

Love to Ed. As ever,
JFT

A little OSFS dirty linen! Saints have been known to steal to help the poor and other causes, but from one another, that's going too far.

He had to pace the floor a few days longer. As Father La Penta's letter indicates, public acclaim was being diverted toward Princess Grace. That is what both prince and priest desired.

Palais de Monaco
February 18, 1957

Dear Joe and Edna:
No thanks! There's only <u>one</u> Canon! We are not a dime a
dozen.
I've written from here congratulations to each and all —
and to the Bishop.
Don't forget that Monsignor Biggins is <u>our</u> cousin.
I'm enjoying stay at the Palace — Grace is wonderful.
Baby sweet. I'm off to Rome the 20th, then back here for the
<u>solemn</u> baptism by Cardinal Tisserant — (baby a bit prema-
ture, baptized privately).
Then I'll go to Paris.
Loving blessing to all
JFT

In response to a letter from brother Joe, Father Tucker is saying he would rather be a Canon than a Monsignor.

Princess Caroline, 8 lbs. 11 ozs., was born on January 23, 1957, 9 months 4 days after the wedding of her parents. Is that a bit premature?

Father Tucker was invited by Prince Rainier to reside at the Palace in the Summer or Fall of 1956. We know that he continued to do so through 1957 but do not know when it terminated.

At last, Father Tucker could say "Mission Accomplished." Monaco had a dedicated Prince, a wonderful Princess, and an heir.

—1 0—
Busy, Busy, Busy

There were few letters to Joe and Edna in 1957. Uncle Francis was both busy and involved with Prince and Princess, as this letter reveals.

OBLATES DE S-FRANCOIS DE SALES
8 AVENUE SAINT CHARLES
MONTE CARLO
23 March 1957

My dear Joe:
What a long time with none but heart to heart correspondence!
I love to write and hate to be prevented from what is to me an
easy and enjoyable task. But with an unending succession of
acts to perform at palace and in parish, and persons of all
descriptions to meet, I'm just sunk. I had Mrs. Kelly on hand
for more than a month, and then John, and then Caroline, and
Grace and Rainier more than ever. Of course, it's nice that
they want me and need me! On the other hand, I can't even get
to Rome as before, and practically have been nowhere out of
Monte Carlo, except for two days at a time twice, since my
return from the States last June.

My health is good. I see to it that I get my rest, another
reason I don't write. But I'm always thinking of all of you and
yours, especially those I don't know and who don't know me
except by name and fame!

The awful part of being famous is that people think
it's synonymous for being rich! You should see the
requests that come to me for loans, handouts and gifts,
such as a wing of a hospital or a whole chapel "Le Pere
Tucker Memorial." It's all very flattering, but what price
glory! I take it naturally in the Amos and Andy stride,

and enjoy being kidded and kidding back.
... LOVE to Ed and All. Always pray for my namesake,
especially, and for all, living and dead.
JFT

For Prince and Princess, falling in love was easier than falling into harmony. Within a few months of the birth of Princess Caroline, Princess Grace was with child again. It took her over two years to find her way as wife, mother, and princess. Her chaplain and friend provided wisdom and comfort during those formative years.

A major event in 1957 for the American Province of the Oblates of Saint Francis de Sales was the opening of their new Salesianum Catholic High School in the Fall. Dedication services were held in May 1957. Canon Tucker came from Monaco to Wilmington, Delaware, to preach at the dedication ceremonies on May 26, 1957. He spoke on education.

In the May 28th edition of the *Wilmington Morning News,* an editorial writer blasted the speech as advocating a breach in the doctrine of separation of Church and State, and was blasted, in turn, by a letter to the Editor.

◆◆◆

DIFFERENT THING?

The editorial titled "Church and State" in the May 28 issue of the Morning News not only did violence to the truth, but, in the process, defamed a native Wilmingtonian whose scholarship, wisdom, and achievements have earned him distinction in this country and in Europe. I refer to the Very Reverend Canon J. Francis Tucker, OSFS, of Monaco, former founder-pastor of Saint Anthony's Church, Wilmington.

I heard Canon Tucker's address at the dedication of the new $3,000,000 Salesianum School last Sunday. Contrary to the editorial, he did not decry separation of church and state, but separation of religion from education, which is not at all the same thing. There are countries today in which there is *separation of church and state, but in which provision is made for religion in education in conformity with the wishes of parents.*

Furthermore, contrary to the editorial, the majority religious view in the United States (Protestant, although only one-third of the population today is affiliated with churches of that group) was, I can testify from personal experience in public schools in New York State, Pennsylvania, New Jersey, and Maryland, taught in the classroom, especially in connection with history, literature, and civics. I have no reason to believe that this is not true today. It was definitely true in my time in such schools, 1917–22, inclusive.

The editorial writer's other points are largely non sequiturs, hardly deserving of a rebuttal. Poor Canon Tucker is not only belabored for what the editorial falsely attributes to him, but for not having discussed related matters in an already extended address. A good many related matters implicit in the editorial also were not stated there as far as that goes.

Viewed as a whole, the lamentable editorial makes me think of an old story told at Chefoo School in China in my boyhood. Several Oxford dons traveling in the Orient visited the boarding school for a few days.

Chatting one evening in the common room, one of the dons was bewailing the "frightfully high price of oysters in the Orient." Another asked idly, "Wonder what's the cause of it?" The third, a jolly fellow, took his glass of port down from his lips long enough to remark cheerily, "Really quite simple, old chap; all due to the low cost of nasturtium seeds."

W.E.F. Smith
Wilmington, May 30

Canon Tucker stayed on in Wilmington well into the month of June. On June 7th, he was the principal speaker at the Commencement exercises for the 1957 graduating class of the Salesianum School at the

Auditorium of the new school building.

During his stay, he made preparations for his next major assignment, a 3-month visit to the Oblates of Saint Francis de Sales mission in Southwest Africa.

Elected a General Councilor of the OSFS in 1949 for a 12-year term, a responsibility he retained when assigned to Monaco by the Vatican, Canon Tucker had a responsibility to be informed, by personal visits, with the worldwide affairs of the OSFS.

One of these was a large mission territory in Southwest Africa assigned to the OSFS by the Vatican. It was staffed by Oblate volunteers from its provinces in Europe and the United States. For many, it was a lifetime commitment.

Canon Tucker journeyed to Southwest Africa in July and remained through September. He sent his brother, Joe, two letters and a postcard during the journey.

23 July 57

Dear Joe:

Trip was fine. Met everywhere by priests and Bishops. Their guest all along route, and treated royally. Health good. Weather ideal. Cool night and morning. Warm but not hot and no humidity — the best vacation I have ever had. A bit tiring, but that's as it should be. At all our stations, there are the good Sisters who do the cooking, a great asset. It will take until mid-September to cover the wide spread of territory — all of the area we serve.

Regards and love to all.
JFT

The large territory — Texas size — assigned to the Oblates is the southern section of southwest Africa overlooking a section of South Africa south of the Orange River.

Uncle Francis was 70 years of age at the time he made this trip.

August 8, 1957 - POST CARD

Joseph A. Tucker
504 W. 19th Street
Wilmington, Del
USA

Doing fine! Visited Father Isenring's grave. What memories.
Am on way to Father Butler. Have covered Bishop
Schlotterback's diocese — 4 times area of Pennsylvania!
Now go to Oblate territory across Orange River-
　Love to all
　JFT

Father Isenring, a pioneer French Oblate, had been a mentor of Canon Tucker at the newly founded Salesianum School in 1905. Father Butler and Bishop Schlotterback were both native Wilmingtonians.

DIOCESE OF KEIMOSS

RT. REVEREND BISHOP
FRANCIS ESSER, OSFS
POST OFFICE BOX 146
SPRINGBOK, C.P.
SPRINGBOK 125

PHONE
SOUTH AFRICA

August 24, 1957

Dear Joe and Edna:
I'm beginning to be proud of myself as an African Missionary.

It's tough in many ways, but so consoling in so many others. The Travel especially I find nerve-racking over deep sand roads with many a rut and dune and at high speed, which is required to master them. It's either skip or skid, so one chooses the lesser evil. Then it's been either Bishop Esser or Schlotterback driving, and what can one say to a Bishop?

I've covered miles and miles from Mission to Mission and their out-stations. Among our Oblate missionaries there are nine different nationalities, which requires all the diplomatic skill the Vatican can import.

Everywhere I'm received by songs and speeches from the children of the Missions, and by meals without end. I've got to watch the diet, especially the water, which is laxative, and the throne-rooms outdoors at sanitary distances from the house, such as we had at 404 West 6th Street, 60 years ago, but not as comfortable nor as near. I've grown since then. It's tough at night by candlelight and dogs announcing the intrusion. But, all in all, the wonderful experience is worth any discomfort to visit all these spots hallowed by our first pioneer missionaries, Father Fromentin as so many I knew, and now managed by the young whom I know also, almost all of them. Naturally they think it's great that the Prince's chaplain should come to them. I'm honored to do so. I feel I've done little in comparison with what I see done by them. 'Twas a great moment when I prayed at Father Isenring's grave. Be back in Europe mid-September.

Love to all,
JFT

The next communication with brother Joe was a post card from Rome dated October 24, 1957.

October 24, 1957

Here reporting on visit to Africa. Was with Holy Father
yesterday — visit successful. Rec'd your letter with appreciated
enclosures before coming here. Father Buckley with us.
Am well and all is O.K. Love to Ed.
    JF Tucker

Canon Tucker's conversations on his trip to Southwest Africa were made not only to his own congregation but to Vatican officials including Pope Pius XII whose health was failing rapidly at that time.

In the Fall of 1957, Joe, Cliff, and Betty made plans for a European trip for their parents, Joe and Edna, that would include a long visit with Brother Francis at Monaco and Rome. The next letter is about that trip.

OBLATES DE S-FRANCOIS DE SALES
8 AVENUE SAINT CHARLES

MONTE-CARLO, LE
MONTE CARLO
19 November 1957

Dear Edna and Joe:
Today is our 4th of July — the National Feast. It brings me a
lot of fatigue, a series of princely ceremonies, functions,
banquets that try men's digestive tracts. The silver lining to all
these clouds was your letter and son, Joe's, delivered on the
eve of the feast.
    My first reaction: isn't Joe's fine gesture a mighty
argument against birth control.
    My second: isn't God good that in His kindly far-seeing

providential way, He detoured Joe from becoming an Oblate.
My third: a full measure of inhibited anticipated joy at the
prospects your coming to Europe hold out for me.

I see no reason why, if everything is timed right, I can't be
with you for most of the itinerary.

I'll be discreet, shall go to a monastery when Edna visits
the Folies Bergere unbeknownst to me, and shall take her to
sanctuaries you have already done honor to, thus allowing you
the bachelor privileges your age calls for.

Try not to tie yourself down to schedule. One must be sure
of hotel reservations but, beyond that, it's better to be free from
tourist trips.

I'm not acquainted with Ireland, England, and Belgium.
But for France, Italy, Monte Carlo, and Switzerland, I can take
charge, if in advance I can get an idea as to the timing.

There will always be, in a pinch, the possibility of housing
overnight, Edna in a convent and you under the protective
custody of a parish priest.

I'll write more later. Must now be off for a priestly Day of
Recollection at the Bishopstead, during which I'll meditate on
ways and means of insuring you spiritually against pitfalls, so
that your son, Joe, may not be even remotely responsible for
the eternal damnation of his parents.

Cheerio, and all my love,
JFT

The Royal banquets were a challenge to Uncle Francis. Each place setting would have a multitude of glasses, china and silverware to be used in proper order during the feast. A reputation could be ruined by selection of the wrong spoon, knife or fork. His solution was elegant. Each guest would have a regally dressed attendant standing behind him/her to provide service. Uncle Francis, using a worthy tip, would arrange with his attendant a set of discreet grunts, etc. to signal which utensil to use. Another Irish solution.

Le Chapelain du Palais
de Lon Altose Serenissime
le Prince de Monaco

December 1957

Thanks, Joe, for your letter and enclosures, which entitle you at the present rate of exchange to four front seats at the midnight Mass. There's a lady here who reserves a chair for her deceased mother — alongside of her. So that takes care of Mother Mac and Mother T.

DON'T PUT OFF your trip! My time can be made to suit yours. I got a letter from Joe, and wrote him. 'Twould be terrible to balk at this initiative. He seems so proud to be in back of it. You parents must please your children too! Edna will fit in queenly with my girl friends who play at the Casino. You need little money and enough jewels to sparkle and to act like a lady. I think it would be nice to start the trip here from CANNES. And not too late in the Summer. Why not arrange for "off-season" travel?
MRY XMAS, Always.
JFT

Christmas Greetings and more about the trip. Our uncle's suggestions to Brother Joe about planning the trip were filed away untouched.

— 11 —
Visitors - 1958

As this letter of February 8, 1958 reveals, our busy Uncle was even busier and ever supportive of the Royal Couple. The February 23 issue of the *Chicago Daily News* had a feature article by Robert Moosel titled "Stork Over Monaco," subtitled "Happy Prince Awaits a Son." In it, Moosel quotes Father Tucker several times based on a personal interview.

Father Francis Tucker, the priest matchmaker, said of Grace: "She has turned that cold mausoleum of a palace into a warm home. Down in their private apartment she and the Prince cook for each other and play house. She brings the baby around for them to see. The people are proud of her. The Prince is proud of her and he is proud of himself for having her. He knows she is a greater attraction of the two and he delights in it.

"He often says, 'You cut the ribbon' or 'You give the prize.' These are things he used to do but is happy to have her the center of attention."

Father Tucker said the people would like to see more of Grace but she has been an expectant mother almost her entire time in Monaco so far and she wants "many children."

Grace and Rainier liked each other when a French magazine introduced them for a publicity photograph. Then Father Tucker prodded destiny into action and so love was born.

Of his part in the story book romance, the Wilmington (Del.) priest remarks somewhat cryptically:

"Perfect matches are made in heaven — safety matches are made by man!"

As I left, he gave me a cigar from the box he is apparently hoarding for the birth of Princess Grace's second baby. On the cellophane wrapper were the hopeful words:

"It's a boy!"

It was a boy. Prince Albert.

◆◆◆

Le Chapelain du Palais
de Lo Altose Serenissime
le Prince de Monaco
February 8, 1958
Dear Joe:

I have been out of my wits trying
to write. "Public relations" weigh
on me so heavily that it's a constant toll of activities — of
being on the run — or staying put at drawn-out affairs at the
palace, where Prince and Princess want me often, or in the
parish, or with OSFSs. I just returned from 5 days at Troyes to
assist at Fiftieth anniversary celebration of Father Brisson's
death. I met him in 1906, and was of some importance at the
celebration.

I got your last letter, don't know where it is among hun-
dreds piled up on my desk since Xmas. I haven't been able to
acknowledge hardly any mail, have no one to secretary for me!

About your trip — You ARE coming, aren't you? And the
sooner the better. Perhaps on a Lourdes pilgrimage, with part-
way arrangements? Whenever such arrangements bring you to
Monte Carlo, we can figure on the rest of your trip from here.

S-P-E-C-I-A-L!!!: I JUST <u>FOUND</u> your letter. The
Vulcania is all right. Is Ed a good sailor? That's a lot of time
on water. I could perhaps meet you at Venice and pilot you
along the rest of the way! We have First Communion here May
11th, so I could be with you before and after that date.

The second route looks good to me: Lisbon to Madrid to
Lourdes. What, for Pete's sake, do you want to go to Trieste
for? ... I got to go.
Love to all.
*   JFT*

Why Trieste, indeed? Because brother Joe was an incurable romantic who would want to visit as many exotic places as possible on any trip. And both Edna and he were "people" persons who would be anxious to meet the friends of their daughter, Betty.

Edna, 68, and Joe, 74, set out to visit brother Francis, 69, and Europe on a 3-month trip. Brother Joe kept a daily log of his April 15–July 21, 1958 journey. Joe and Edna arrived in Monte Carlo the evening of May 7th and remained there until June 2nd, except for a side trip to Lourdes. They then left for a leisurely trip to Rome, arriving there on June 7th. Father Francis (Joe and Edna always referred to Uncle Francis as Father Francis) arrived in Rome June 9th and stayed with them until June 18th. They left for Switzerland, Germany, Belgium, France, and then home. The following are excerpts from Brother Joe's log.

May 8
MONTE CARLO

At 11 a.m. with Father Charles La Penta, we went to a ceremony at the French Consulate. The Prince and Princess drove up with guards and music — a real Hollywood sight. Then with Father Francis we drove to the Palais. He went in. Then the Count D'Alliere came out and invited us in for cocktails. We met the Countess — charming, regular people. Afterwards we met others in the Palace. Dined that evening with Father Francis at Hotel de Paree's outside pavilion. Great!

♦♦♦

May 11
MONTE CARLO

We attended church at Saint Charles 3 times. Dined at the rectory for lunch with Father Francis, 7 priests and the Countess Dalcon — 1st Communion Day and Confirmation in the p.m. Dined late at a little restaurant and spent the evening in the little park facing the Casino. Then to our very nice and comfortable hotel.

✦✦✦

MAY 18
MONTE CARLO

*Saint Charles for Mass, then back to our hotel where we had a
grand view from our room balcony of the Grand Prix auto
races lasting 3-1/2 hours. Father La Penta, Father Looney and
another French priest were our guests. Father Francis sat in
the stands with the Princeand guests.*

✦✦✦

MAY 24TH
MONTE CARLO

*Father Francis called us. Said he had invited the Prince and
Princess to dinner on the 26th. We were to be ready by 6 p.m.
Informal. We spent the p.m. at the Monte Carlo Beach and
Club. Nice bus ride. Had a sidewalk dinner near the casino.*

✦✦✦

My dear Mary and Joseph:
*How wonderful to receive my Mother's Day Card on the very
day we are so far away from home. Thank you so much.
Monte Carlo is so different and beautiful. I am writing this
and looking out the hotel window (Balmoral Hotel) at the
Mediterranean and the lights in the Palace, beautiful sight.
Had lunch today at the Casino Cafe with Father Francis;
really, your mother and dad are living in another world and
enjoying every minute of it, thanks to you wonderful children,
hard to believe it is true. Tomorrow evening Father Francis is
having a spaghetti dinner for the Prince and Princess, Count
and Countess Dolliere (the Countess is Grace's Lady in*

waiting) and ourselves. Father Francis is telling us how to act, etc, and of course we are teasing him. I have, too, for he told the Count and Countess while we were having cocktails in their apt. the other day that I drink a lot, so I have to get back at him. I am having mine kissed (remember I said hands). Sent your folks cards, Mary. Think we will be having to go to Rome next week. This rest sure has been wonderful for we sure have traveled.

Met some nice people on the boat, I had canasta friends, still hearing from them. Your Dad Kissing a lot of Hands. Kiss the children for us. Will write again.

Love to you all
Mother

✦✦✦

MAY 26TH
MONTE CARLO

Spent the a.m. getting a hair trim, etc. Then left the hotel at 5:30 for Father Francis. He briefed us how to act. At 7 p.m. the Royal Couple arrived.

After introductions, most informal, and a cocktail, we went to the dining room. At the table sat Father Francis, Edna and myself on either side. Then the Prince and Princess and the Count and Countess D'Allieres. Spaghetti with chicken, salads, wine and champagne was served. Everything was delicious.

The Princess asked for seconds. So we all followed. We all talked and whiled away about 2 hrs at the table. We all adjourned to a small game room. All played a miniature game of pool. Had cocktails, talked.

The Prince and Princess left at 1 a.m. All had a most enjoyable evening. And we didn't feel like commoners. Just Americans.

Uncle Francis must have been pleased that Prince and Princess would spend six hours at his dinner party. The repartee must have been exhilarating. Prince, Princess, Priest, and sister-

in-law all were masters of humor both straight and sly. Brother Joe could roar with laughter, seemingly from his soul.

A little family lore. After the introductions Father Tucker asked what would his guests like to drink. There was an awkward pause. Then Edna said: "I would like a beer." The Prince said: "I would like a beer too." Ice broken, party on.

At one repartee during the evening, Edna said to brother-in-law Francis: "I should have married you." The Prince loved it and did not forget it.

To one grandchild, Edna was known as the grandmother who drank beer. The story: Grandma was a frail lady who took a variety of medicines to counter the aches and pains of life with husband, Joe. As a lady she would have nothing to do with so common a beverage as beer. One evening, while in distress, she was persuaded to drink a beer. Miraculous relief! Away went the medicines; in came the beer. Two a day only — afternoon and evening.

MAY 29TH
MONTE CARLO

With Father Francis we went to the Palace, at the request of the Princess, to meet her children.

The Princess brought them to us in their private living room. Little Caroline is darling.

After the visit, Father Francis showed us through both state and other sections of the Palace including the Chapel. We saw many of their wedding gifts. Had a lovely day.

◆◆◆

MAY 30 – JUNE 1

Shopped Monte Carlo in the a.m. and 6:30 p.m. with Father

Francis, we, at his request, visited Prince Pierre at his villa and had cocktails. He was very friendly. Nice visit!

On the 1st we attended Mass at Saint Charles. Went to the Palace grounds for lunch and back to Saint Charles for Confirmation service. In the evening to the casino. We went through the various rooms, but only played the coin machines. Lost, of course. It is a very beautiful place.

<u>A Thank You Note From Prince Pierre</u>
Many many thanks for your lovely flowers and congratulations to an old man!

I was deeply touched by your very kind gesture and thought.

All best wishes for a happy continuation of your trip.

Prince Pierre

The travelers left in the morning for Rome, with an overnight in Genoa and 4 nights in Florence, arriving in Rome June 7th for a 12-day stay, joined by Father Francis for 10 of them. The following are excerpts from the log.

JUNE 8
ROME

Father Francis arrived and took us to Saint Peter's. We saw the Pope at his Vatican window. Then toured Saint Peter's. Went to the roof; then also the Treasure rooms. Then, driven by Signor Mario, we went to Frascatis for lunch. Then to Castle Gondolfo, the Pope's summer residence. Drove through his garden, visited the castle. Then to Villa Altiery at Albano, the Oblate Novitiate. Then back to Rome. Stopped at a German beer garden for beer.

In the evening, to Via Verdiato just to sight see.

♦♦♦

JUNE 11
ROME

With Father Francis, we went to Saint Peter's at 11 a.m. for the weekly public audience with the Pope. We saw his entrance, listened to him speak in 8 languages, received his blessing, kissed his ring.

There were 20,000 people present. After, we went to Saint Mary Maggiore's. Then back to the hotel and dinner with General of Oblates.

♦♦♦

JUNE 15

Sunday — heard Mass at Jesuit Church. Father Francis given 2 tickets for Papal Audience in Vatican. We went.

Then to Saint Paul's Basilica — then 3 coins in a fountain.

To Blessed Sacrament Church — Lunch at 12 Apostles, then 2 more churches and back to hotel.

Uncle Francis sent this June 16 from Rome.

Le Chapelain du Palais
de Lon Altose Serenissime
le Prince de Monaco
ROME
June 16

Dear Doctor and Mary:
The Arabian Nights, the Three Musketeers, the Innocents Abroad, Robinson Crusoe, etc., pale into insignificance when

compared to "JOE & EDNA SEE EUROPE."

Their illustrious brother & brother-in-law has lost some of his lustre in the shadow of the reflected glory of their charm and warmth.

The details of their trip tell nothing of the impression created by them on all and sundry persons, from Pope and Prince to lowlier folk, whom they met.

I am very proud of them both. They've outdone themselves in every field of human endeavor, physical endurance, moral courage, diplomatic skill, religious fervor, and financial wizardry.

I'm very proud of you, too, and grateful for the inspiration of it all.

Love to all
JFT

And the following excerpt from a letter from Mother Edna dated June 18.

"Will have to tell you about Rome when we see you. It has been the most wonderful ten days of our lives due to Father Francis. He has had us everywhere. The audience was the big thrill.

Can't write much. Father Francis leaves for Monte Carlo tonight. We leave early tomorrow morning for Geneva, Switzerland."

Uncle Francis did not breathe a sigh of relief as he trained back to Monte Carlo. He had a wonderful time with his two closest friends. He sent them this letter to reach them in Paris.

OBLATS DE ST-FRANCOIS DE SALES
MONTE-CARLO le
8, AVENUE SAINT-CHARLES
MONTE-CARLO
6 July, 1958

My dear Edna and Joe:
I got all your cards and so could follow you on your trip.
Delighted to know that all was and is well. I sent a telegram to
Hotel Union at Lucerne, just to say: "CARDS RECEIVED
HAPPY ALL IS WELL CHEERIO-FRANCIS" Thought I had
timed it right to reach, but got back a return:
"Changed Address."
    NOW, when you get home, lose no time to send a Thank
You card, on aristocratic stationery, with the Tucker-McJilton
coat of Arms, to
    H.S.H. PRINCE PIERRE OF MONACO
    Villa Saint Martin
    Monaco Principality
with something like this on it — "Your Highness: Among the
most prized souvenirs of our trip to Europe is the exquisite
kindness Your Highness did us by the delightful reception
accorded us with Father Francis.
    Our children and grandchildren share the pride and gratitude
such honor brought this branch of Father Francis' family.
    We remain eternally indebted.
    Edna and Joseph Tucker."
    You, Edna, write it, and sign for both, as indicated. That's
how Princess Grace does it for Her and His!
    And then send one to:
    Their Serene Highnesses,
    The Prince and Princess of Monaco
    Le Palais
    MONACO PRINCIPALITY.

"Your Serene Highnesses:

Father Francis' elder brother and junior sister-in-law have brought home with them among the most cherished souvenirs of their visit to Europe, the exquisite kindness Your Highnesses showed them, both at Saint Charles and at the Palace. The thrill our children and grandchildren share most with us is that of having seen Princess Caroline in Her own home and that of Her Royal little Brother.

We are very grateful and so happy to have witnessed how much "at home" our dear Father Francis is in the lovely country that has adopted him.

With all our thanks,
Respectfully,
Edna and Joseph Tucker."
Then, send a card to:
Most Reverend D. Balducelli
49 Via Dandolo, Rome Italy.
Cav. Alfred Novelli, and Cav. Mario Pranzetti
Vatican City.
and
Father Rory O'Sullivan
College Saint Michel, Annecy. H. Savoy, France.

We are not sure really whether this letter was "tongue in cheek" or not. We suspect it was a spoof at royal protocol. Letters were sent, as requested.

We have no record of other letters to Joe and Edna in 1958. His beloved Church was about to be shaken to its foundations. The ailing Pius XII died in 1958, leaving a Church ready for reform.

Pope John XXIII appointed Canon Tucker's friend, Cardinal Tardini, to be Vatican Secretary of State and assigned him the task of planning and organizing the Second Vatican Council.

— 12 —
Septuagenarian 1959 to 1960

Under a full head of steam, Canon J. Francis Tucker, OSFS, reached age 70 on January 8, 1959. In the 1959–1960 years he made several trips to the United States in which he was able to briefly visit Joe and Edna. Consequently, there are fewer letters to them in those years.

August 17, 1959.

Dear Joe:

Yours of 25th at hand today, on my return from Annecy where I spent ten days on retreat, alone as I wanted it, away from the whirl of the work in which I live, tiring and annoying. Only last night at dinner with Prince and Princess in their country ranch, we were talking about Edna's repartees at table in Saint Charles. Thanks for enclosure, and for news of families, etc. ... You are a happy old pair, you and Edna, ruling over more generations than the Sovereign of Monaco. In spiritual terms, Francis is worth more to all of us than all of us are to him. 'Tis God's way. My health is good. Cranky, that's all! Get soothed with a gin-tonic. I'm going to Ireland to help install the new Papal Nunzio, Monsignor Riberi, a boy from Saint Charles' parish. ... The news from Saint Anthony's suits me. Love to all.

> *Ever,*
> *JFT*

This letter indicates that he continued to be close to Grace and Rainier. It also contains a reference to basic Catholic Christian belief about each person's personal journey toward salvation.

John Francis Tucker, the fourth child of Joe and Edna Tucker and Uncle Francis' namesake, was hospitalized permanently in 1947 afflicted with a severe schizophrenia, an illness resulting from near fatal bouts in his teen years with ulcerous spleen disorders and lumbar polio over a 4-year period. Born deaf in February, 1928, he never had robust health. As the first signs of his namesake's mental illness appeared, Uncle Francis arranged for him to attend a renowned school for the deaf, hoping that a new environment might be a catalyst for recovery. It did not succeed.

Joe and Edna were devastated by their son's fate. How, then, to accept it spiritually?

In this letter Father Francis states, "In spiritual terms, Francis is worth more to all of us than all of us are to him. 'Tis God's way." In September 1949, he had written, "At all the shrines I have visited, I've prayed for Francis. I do so every day at Mass. I'm persuaded that he is for all of us a blessing in disguise — the type of victim that stays the hand of God against the rest of us."

And on January 3, 1950, "I pray for Francis everywhere always. He is still the greatest blessing the family has and will be higher up than any of us in heaven."

A true evaluation of a Christian life must be in spiritual terms. There is no unworthy life unless it be that of an unrepentant sinner. The more worthy the life, the more the sacrificial demands made upon it, demands that, if accepted, are blessings rather than punishment. Father Francis was saying that his nephew was called, in a vocational sense, to lead a life of deprivation for all humanity — a vocational life, in the sense that cloistered religious have chosen and consider themselves called to a life of prayer. Francis' life is a prayer. Has he accepted it?

When his illness began, Francis was resentful of his deafness, the removal of his spleen, his life situation. It expressed itself in overt hostility. However, when the moment came to accept treatment in a mental hospital, he went without rancor, in fact, willingly and, to the writer's knowledge, never complained about being there nor expressed a wish not to be there.

An aside! Because of his severe respiratory and other illnesses, for years Francis had been confined to a hospital within a hospital. On a visit to Francis a few years ago, the writer noted that he was very well cared for. One nurse said, "He is our baby." But he seemed sad. Another nurse said. "That could be because Mrs. Trippett is away on vacation. I hope she is not here when he passes away." Francis had a mother's love. He died of pneumonia May 20, 1992.

Sept. 3, 1959

Dear Joe,
I'm here with the new Papal Nunzio to Ireland, Monsignor
Riberi, a native son of the parish, Saint Charles, Monte Carlo.
He is a wonderful man, only 61 and 25 yrs. a Bishop. In
Vatican diplomacy all the while: Africa, China, Formosa, and
now "the Isle of Saints."
    I seem to be well known to the Irish. They speak of me as
"the holy priest who helped to put a Kelly on the Throne" —
and they are showering me with receptions and Irish tea
parties. It's a wonderful change from the "sunny spot for shady
people."
    I'm seeing a bit of the land and enjoying it immensely.
Hope to be back to Monaco about the 15th. Love to Edna and
all.
    JFT

Father Francis was thrilled to be visiting Ireland.

Sept. 14, 1959

Dear Joe and Edna:
Yours of Aug. 29th read yesterday, Sept. 13th, on my return
from IRELAND.
    I went to Ireland officially accompanying Monsignor
Riberi, a native son of my parish, just named Papal Nunzio to
Dublin. I was received with all the hurrahs meant for Grace
KELLY. Dined twice with DeValera and Cosgrave and
past-president Shemas O'Kelly, and the Cardinal of Armagh
and Archbishop of Dublin, and down the line.
    I took off 3 days to visit Thurles in Tipperary County,
whence come the Hickeys. I found in the parish church

159

*Grandpa Edward Butler Hickey's baptism register, 1817, with
those of Michael and John, doubtless Grand-Uncles. When this
was known, keys of the city and open doors everywhere for the
famous greatgrandson of the soil. And all Irish newspapers
heralding the tidings of national joy! Two genealogists offering
their research work gratis to establish further information, and
numerous Hickeys claiming cousinship with me! I wanted to
visit Waterford, where at Saint John's Edward B. received
minor orders. And, according to the story of his daughter, Mary
Ellen Elizabeth, was disowned by the pater-familias for not
persevering, about which I am dutifully grateful. Have you any
items on this? About the Tuckers from Donnegal, I have nothing to go by — that research document you sent me being
surely of a wrong branch. Wonder if Ellen Devine has any faint
memory of things her mother might have related, or the
McDonoughs or Reardons or the late Nell and Margaret
Tucker girls' living kin?*

Try to find out.

*To date, I've always been indifferent about the matter, for
fear we might have had unpleasant antecedents. My memories
of Edward B. are that he was gentleman and scholar and a
bear that when wife No. 2, Maria, was giving me a lump of
sugar with whiskey on it for a cold I had at the age of four, her
husband who, according to his daughter, Mary Ellen Elizabeth,
observed the vow of nuptial chastity towards Maria, scolded
her for teaching me bad habits. The course of history has
proven that perhaps he was right. He taught me Latin when I
was eight, and did me the favor of dying before I had to perform the humiliating task which my three brothers before me
did perform before First Communion, namely to ask his pardon
for sins we had never committed.*

*Don't let Edna ask me to look up the McJilton records —
suspicion was cast on her family when her father, driving his*

Ford, deliberately blocked the progress on a public highway of President Wilson's auto. Of course, the remaining Huttons can take care of the maternal side.

Thanks for the enclosures, always deeply appreciated. And love to the four generations of the Hickeys!

Ever,

JFT

P.S. Let Ed know about this

JFT

So Father Francis and his brothers (Joe, Ed, and Bill) are verifiably Irish on the Hickey side, with considerable temperament inherited from that "bear," old grandpa Hickey. But were the Tuckers Irish or, God forbid, English?

Tucker is an English name. However, the name O'Tuachaer is the name of two distinct septs, one of the Ely-O'Carrol territory and the other in Ulster of North Connacht. In both locations the name became Toker, Tooker and even Tucker. But Uncle Francis was not able to make a genealogical connection.

Grandnephew Bill, son of brother Bill, made a strong case for an English Tucker genealogy. He writes:

Nice try! Uncle Francis went down that same route but Hickey is as Irish as it gets. It all came apart when we met that guy in the Protestant Church in Dover, Delaware, and your father (Joe) and he made out that their fathers were brothers. (Later I met a Tucker from that side who looked just like Uncle Ed. His name was Ed Tucker, too. And I found out later that he met a girl from Saint Anthony's and was converted to Catholic and married in Saint Anthony's.) That meeting substantiated Margaret Durney's account of the two brothers from Virginia who came up to work on a dam in Maryland. I guess you wonder how would she know. It seems our grandfather dated Margaret's mother seriously before he married old Mary Hickey. Durney gave up on him because he wasn't Catholic. Hickey converted him. That grandmother of ours was a very persuasive person.

◆◆◆

161

It was best for Uncle Francis to have been "indifferent about the matter for fear we might have had unpleasant antecedents." A confounding note is that Uncle Francis' father's sister was also Catholic. Let's settle for American, which is the truth of it.

Nov. 27, 1959

Dear Joe:

Got your letter of 24th two minutes ago, and hasten to say that Cholly Knickerbocker is a liar — the Begum was never in sight at our Sovereign's visit to Paris. Princess Grace, according to ALL French papers, was Superb in beauty, bounty, and behavior. I was with them at Rome. Cholly Knickerbocker is again an arch-liar in his remarks about that visit: Italian papers reported that at the Grand Reception given by the Prince, "Everybody that was anybody in Rome was there," and the same people who vied to do honor to the venerable chaplain of the Court (that's ME) told me that Rome rarely sees the equal of that reception. Not one request was made from our side to get "Rome's smart set" to throw parties for the Grimaldis. On the contrary, time wouldn't permit us to accept the flow of bids addressed to the palace for receptions to our beloved couple.

YES, I've been over-busy, beyond endurance. The new job at the Monaco Embassy to the Holy See gives me important and consuming work and worry. And I really get tired. I spent Thanksgiving getting off my Xmas mail so I wouldn't have to at the last minute buy air-mail stamps. Your enclosure squares me with the P.O. for the ordinary stamps. Very grateful for the boost, but please apply all surplus loose change to our grand-children. Wish I was with you all last Thursday, and more so do I regret my absence at Xmas. I simply can't get away.

The Prince and Princess often ask for "Joe and Edna."
Cheerio,
JFT

Father Francis, as chaplain, was expected to participate in many social affairs of the Royal Court.

His assignment as an ecclesiastical counselor to the Monaco Embassy was a fourth job. Why it was important we do not know.

Feb. 25, 1960

My dear Joe and Edna:
This too long delay in writing is due to the fact that I can't get to write at all, always on the go. Rome taking up half my time — Monaco the other half — and in between halves, visits to Fribourg, Switzerland, Troyes, with chores to do for Oblates, the Prince, the Vatican, my parish, and scores of outside jobs wished on me by all sorts of persons.

I feel it too — a thing you can't estimate because you have your better half to do most of the work and worry. How often have I wished that you had been a priest and me Edna's partner! If I recall correctly, Edna said something in harmony with this idea to the Prince at table in my rectory, didn't she? Of course, I would never have been at a loss for partnership, what with the many strewn along my path: Joan Mulvena, Nell Ford, Kay Bowe, and even more tender aspirants such as kept Mother Tucker seconded by Mother Mac in constant prayer and maternal vigilance.

No use of me saying I'll get over this year, I can't know in advance. I HOPE to.

Love to all,
JFT

More tongue in cheek. He did get home to attend the funeral of Grace's father, John Kelly, who died of cancer June 20, 1960 at Philadelphia, Pennsylvania.

A death of great consequence to the Roman Catholic Church and to Father Tucker personally was that of his friend Cardinal Tardini, Vatican Secretary of State, in 1960.

July 30, 1960

Dear Joe and Edna:
Prince and Princess and Prince Pierre were asking for you
while recalling your visit to us here in Monaco. I really en-
joyed that part of the funerals (Mr. Kelly's and Father Smith's)
which brought me near you and the subdivisions of the Klan,
Cliff's and Betty's — sorry to have missed Joe's! The Coach
from Billy and Bobby's school came to see me. Glad I was able
to be nice to them. Here in Rome for OSFS matters, and back
again tonight to Monaco. All is well in both places and I think
it's good to get away just to make these great and little ones
miss me! It's my turn to be missing all of you — and how I
do!!!
> *Love to all,*
> *JFT*

In a press interview, Father Francis reported that the Royal Couple
had received a cablegram over the personal signature of Pope John
XXIII offering condolences on the death of Princess Grace's father.

Nov. 15, 1960

Dear Joe:
I've been wanting to write but kept on the go entirely too much
and too often for an oldster like me.
> *I had to organize, manage, and finance the Jubilee*
celebrations of Fathers General and Lichtle, the Treasurer. A
lot of running around Rome, France, and Switzerland to get the
boys in line — no easy task. In so doing, however, it seems I
stirred up some thoughts and wishes among the brethren that I
might make a good General. This prospect has set me studying
the tactics of Jack Kennedy. Since he was greatly helped by his
brother, the thought comes to me that perhaps you could help

campaign for me; over here, of course, and, as the female appeal is strong, even where it shouldn't be, Edna might be an asset, and I'm sure she wouldn't object, since you both know the territory to be canvassed. Germany should be easy and Italy too, with the slogan that you two gave and gladly gave your flesh and blood, though in other peoples' bodies down to the 4th generation, to the cause of the Germans andItalians (6 votes). I figure you could get 2 votes from Holland — surely Reisinger's from Austria. Switzerland is doubtful, though Edna looks a bit like Father Hartmann's deceased sister, which might bring one vote. And then France, though the great handicap there is that most of the Fathers know that you and Edna went to the Folies Bergere, and think that's a smear on me. There remains the African Missions and USA—? Tom Lawless is campaigning actively for Bill Buckley, so nobody can complain if you and Edna come out for me!

Love to all — what's Betty's address?
JFT

Father Francis clearly was "blowing smoke" in this letter. He had no intention of running for Superior General of the Oblates of Saint Francis de Sales. But religious orders are both democratic and political at election time. Knowing whose side God is on is always after the fact.

Dec. 8, 1960

Dear Edna and Joe:
Sure some news you sent me about Ed.
I'm writing him for Xmas, of course without any mention. One would think that Ed had taken sufficient antiseptic to immunize the throat of a giraffe! However, one of our holiest Oblates, old past-Superior General, Father Dufour, now 84, has the same malady. They say it occurs frequently enough

165

among oldsters regardless of the intake of holy water or blue flame!

So happy to be a Grand-Uncle for the fortieth time! I've lost all count, but must say that the Tucker-McJilton mustard seed has sure spread out unto a mighty tree! It's evident that you two shall live on through centuries to come and world without end!

Thanks, Edna, for the addresses — I'm sending Xmas cards.

BUT NOW, I am asking you to divide the enclosure among the Tucker-McJilton branches, Betty, Joe, Cliff, for the kiddies. I mean don't send them money, but you buy something for them and ship it, which I can't very well do. AND KEEP Francis' share for such something he may use. AND NO nonsense about this! When Anna Graham and Mrs. McHugh were here a month ago, they were more than generous to me, so I can help Ed and his crew a bit, and our brother Bill's brood.

Of course, Joe, you are free to deduct a sum sufficient to buy some beautifying products for Edna, if you judge it helpful or necessary.

I'm all right. Slowing up a bit, yet being driven like a willing horse. I've got two fine men here with me, Jim Boston and Tom O'Connell. They do a great job. There's also an Italian, who is sick and unable to do hard work.

I hope to get to USA in '61 for my 50 years a priest.

MERRY XMAS and love to all,

JFT

Father Francis had learned from brother Joe that brother Ed was afflicted with a serious throat disorder. The reference to antiseptic is to Ed's habit of spending weekends with alcoholic rather than religious spirits. And, once again, he wants to be Santa's helper for 40grandnieces and grandnephews.

In the 1959–1960 period, Father Francis made few references to his work as counselor to Prince Rainier. What he may have said to brother Joe in private we do not know since Joe was tight-lipped about the few such confidences that he may have received. But that Father Tucker was involved as a senior advisor on matters diplomatic and political is certain. He may have reached the peak of his influence during those years.

Christmas, 1960

Dear Mary and Doctor:
My proud and grateful and heartfelt congratulations on the happy event that makes of me a thirty-three degree Grand-Uncle.

And a word to say that I asked the Senior member of our family and his lady-in-waiting to relay to the Branches of their family tree the results of the shopping I asked them to do for Santa Claus' younger brother, who happens to be ME. I just want to check on the old folks and to delegate Kevin to give you all my blessing (on bended knee) ...
JFT

This Christmas card was sent to Uncle Francis' nephew, Joe, and his wife, Mary. In his own bombastic style he refers to the birth of grand-nephew Stephen, the last of the brother Joe's line of grandchildren.

— 13 —
The Promenade - 1961

"Whew! What a difference! What is going on here?" The American tourist once again had returned to Monaco and was visiting with his Monacoan friend.

"The Prince is having his way. That is what is going on here," was the reply.

"I can see that there is a building boom, much of it right here in La Condomine. Highrises where villas used to be. How do you feel about that?"

"Many of us are unhappy about it. It's more than villas that we are losing. Our ways of living are changing with it. More people, new people. More activity, new activity. But we are prospering from it, and we Monacoans are still the real citizens of Monaco."

"That's what's important, isn't it? But tell me more about the changes."

"The Prince's railroad underground project will be completed soon. We now know he was right. It will mean a lot economically and will remove an eye-sore. And if you haven't seen it already, you can observe the land reclamation project to the east of The Rock. We will add land needed for a light industry industrial park. We are enthusiastic about that. Also, you will see that not all of the highrises are apartments. Some are offices for the many businesses the Prince hopes to attract here. One attraction is the tax-free status they will have."

"That has been one of the Prince's main goals all along, hasn't it? In some ways he seems more Top Executive than Prince."

"Seems, yes! Really, no! He is the Prince, and he doesn't let us forget it. And that's the way we want him, no matter what we might say in private. But his plan is working. He wants Monaco to be much more than a tourist-plus-gambler spot. In fact, other than for its Monte Carlo mystique, we could do without the casino. But we won't. It's as much an anchor as is The Rock."

"So times are good, as we would say. It seems that the whole world saw the wedding. That whole affair was a great surprise."

"Surprise, indeed! We were surprised, stunned, shocked, exhilarated. The engagement announcement was incredible, unbelievable. There had not been even a rumor in the rumor capital of the world. We are expert Prince watchers but he fooled us completely. He kept telling us to stop nagging him about getting married."

"How did you feel about it once you were sure it was true?"

"We were very happy that the Prince was to be married at last. You know why. But we always have misgivings. Who was this young woman? What was she like? Would she give up her acting career? Our consolation was that the Prince's chaplain was involved. We knew that he would try to keep the Prince from making a mistake."

"Well, it seems that he has so far. The wedding was a grand affair, wasn't it?"

"It could have been. It was planned to be a Catholic celebration. But the news media and the human trash that accompanies it did their best to turn it into a circus. We have never seen anything like that collection of 1800 amoral, cynical, self-worshiping, arrogant, ignorant chameleons in our checkered history. They insulted us. Took over our streets. Had no respect for our property. Believe me, I lived through our occupation by the Nazis in World War II without being trodden on like that human plague did. Thank God they left as quickly as they came."

"My God, my friend, was it really that bad?"

"Yes, it was. What was most embittering was the total lack of respect for the union that the Prince and Princess were forming. Perhaps God was punishing us for not having more respect for it ourselves."

"I am sure there must be some happy memories for all of you in spite of all the hoopla! By the way, I am curious as to what it cost the Principality to host the wedding."

"About $500,000 in expenditures. But revenues more than covered it. We believe that the Prince earned about $450,000 from the sale of commemorative stamps alone."

"Now tell me about the Princess. She is a Princess, isn't she?"

"We love her, both as a person and a Princess. She is genuine, real. There is nothing, as you Americans would say, 'phony' about her. We were skeptical at first, for she seemed aloof. But we soon learned that she was pregnant, and that had its side effects. The Prince is not good enough for her, but what man would be? I sound like her father or uncle, do I not? But that's the way I feel. She is ours, our family."

"And the Prince?"

"He is both the same but different. He is the same ruler, the same boss. Still imperious at times. Still ambitious for the Grimaldis and

Monaco. Yet he is madly in love. That is different. We think he is now more sure of himself. And she is the reason."

"And the children?"

"Ah! We had selfish reasons for wanting the Prince to have heirs. The survival of the Principality probably depends on it. But they are beautiful children. A little spoiled? Perhaps! We know that they have 'first call' on the time of their busy parents. We expect that there will be more children, though it is rumored that the Princess has had two miscarriages."

"A few years ago the American press carried feature items about the royal chaplain, Canon Tucker. Is he still here?"

"Very much so! We marvel at his energy, for he is now 70 years old. He is very influential with the Prince and Princess. A trusted advisor. He is very popular with us Monagasques for his work as pastor of Saint Charles Church. He has improved conditions greatly for our children and us. Through him we have a direct voice to the Prince, not filtered by politicians and 'uppers,' some of whom are very jealous of him. And they can have slanderous tongues. We understand he is now an advisor to our legation in Rome. Another job."

"The good father is bound to run out of steam sooner or later. Since my last visit, I have heard of conflicts between the Prince and the National Assembly, including some interesting family gossip."

"There is some truth to the gossip. Princess Antoinette, the Prince's older sister, married a Mr. Rey, our chief protagonist against the Prince's policies, no matter what. Rey, the head of the National Assembly, is thought to have tried to have the Princess declared the legal heir to the throne, without success. In any case, the Prince has not backed off from any of his goals. He is a very tough man, possibly too tough. Family tensions have been reduced largely because of Princess Grace's influence. And there is Onassis. As you know, his money and influence supported the Principality greatly a few years ago. But now the Prince and he are in conflict about policies concerning the casino and the development of Monaco. We don't know how that will turn out. The 'grapevine' reports that the Princess is a calming influence on this also."

"My friend, when we first met you were worried about the Principality's future. At our next meeting you were still worried. What do you Monagasques worry about now?"

"Oh! We have an active list. I will mention a few. We are now being invaded by many French expatriates from Algeria. Many are here to dodge France's taxes. That could lead to trouble.

"Then there is our imperious neighbor, Charles De Gaulle. He may want to conquer Monaco as he talks France back to glory.

"And many of us feel that the Prince is over-building. But the biggest worry of all, Hollywood. The Princess has lost none of her beauty and charm. What she has done for our tourist trade tells us what an attraction she is."

"Thank you for your candor, my friend. Once more, I'll bet the Prince. Adieu."

— 14 —
Decisions 1961 to 1962

Father Tucker celebrated his 72nd birthday on January 8, 1961. Later in that year he would celebrate the 50th anniversary of his ordination as a priest. Aside from the health of family members, his major concern was for the future of the Oblates of Saint Francis de Sales and the winding down of his own career. There were surprises.

Jan. 9, 1961

Dear Joe:
Your red letter greetings of the 3rd reached me on Sat. 7th, and so brought the old home touch to my seventy-second!

And don't tell me that you are only a beginner in the art of typing, spacing, punctuating, and all the mechanical maneuvering of your Smith-Corona!

What a RELIEF for sore eyes!

And STOP sending back the change I sent for the third generation! Tell Ed I did not omit the Smuckers nor Doll this time. I never forget them, but sin only by omission.

About Ed —it worries me a lot. Please do keep me informed. Doctors can gauge fairly accurately the limit of endurance of a patient. I want to see Ed before he reaches that limit. Naturally, if the inevitable occurs, I shall come over. I did for Grace Kelly's father, my official position obligated me to this. But blood is thicker than water, and I shall certainly come over for my own. This statement is not to be interpreted in the sense that I pray for the happy and speedy release from the tyranny that Edna has had to endure from you since the fatal morn at dawn-light in Saint Patrick's when I sealed the bond of union between your then virginal souls. As a matter of fact, I feel that Prince Pierre would expect Edna and you to lead my funeral cortege from Saint Charles to the Palace, to

*the Cathedral, and thence to Pan American for my last flight
to Saint Anthony's! Pierre would expect Edna to be his
house-guest through the mourning, while you and Rainier
would stay around the bier in the palace, perhaps with cousin
Bill Jeandell. Doubtless Edna would want Cousin Ellen, the
Duchess of Haddon Hall, for her lady-in-waiting. And Nancy
can stay in the Convent of the Dames de Saint Maur.*

*It's great to be able to meet death smiling but that's only
when it's your own. So let me know how things are in Ed's
case.*

*My campaign is all backstage so far. All I do want is to see
the present incumbent OUT.*

LOVE to all
JFT

More family whimsy! Brother Ed was terminally ill. Since Ed had
not been a churchgoer, his brother Francis was anxious to revive his
spirituality at that most critical time. The last sentence refers to his
campaign to prevent Father Balducelli from getting a second 12-year
term as Superior General of the Oblates of Saint Francis de Sales.

Jan. 30, 1961

Dear Fellow-stenog:
*Yours of the 19th reached me in bed, where from that date till
today, I have been ridden with a heavy dose of bronchitis,
intestinal grippe, and old age.*

*The Doctor has come daily till today. A bit weak and
unwilling, after eight days of being fed like a rabbit on carrots,
boiled lettuce, and like a Chinaman on rice! And medication by
way of all the openings of the human frame. The rest was
needed, and I feel better. Kept thinking, dreaming about ED —
and praying. Waiting, I don't deny, for such information as you
might have to send, whether suddenly or at leisure.*

I DO want to come over — in case!

Have just written to young Bill to relay my words to his Dad. You, too, tell Ed I am rooting for him.

I had to miss all the festivities of the National Patron Saint's Day, Saint DEVOTA, a virgin-lady who by all odds became the patron of this land of adultery. Was just as glad to miss and BE MISSED!

Had to miss also the Consistory in Rome for the new Cardinals, including Saint Louis, whom I know! But that was just so much and so many lire saved.

Terribly sorry to learn about MARY. But that's only a signal for Joe to stop. Young Eddie, you know, kept going even after Peg came back from the Sanitarium the first time. What will Joe do? There's only one way out: Polygamy! As the Jesuits say: The END justifies the means. But Mary will be all right! I always thought she was the nun type and, naturally, a bit of a shock must come sooner or later. So be it! Worst thing about the situation is Mary's Mother-in-Law can have little sympathy for the case, because she was the marrying-type, Grade A. Jim Grant told me that Edna was a temptation to the most chaste seminarians in Baltimore, way before you fell! GOD BLESS YOU, Edna, for it — I mean, for rescuing Joe, my brother, and with him, the rest of the Tucker clan, me included, from dismal despair.

I'm writing to Joe.

Love,

Brother-stenog

Another bout with the flu! A yearly occurrence.

Mary, the daughter-in-law of Joe and Edna, had a severe post-partum breakdown after the birth of her fourth child, Stephen. Father Tucker had both sympathy for and understanding of the problems women can have in childbearing and rearing. His reference to polygamy is face-tious, as is his comment about sister-in-law Edna. But his mention of "stop" was not. He wanted sexual discipline in men based on a concern for what was best for their wives.

Brother Ed died within two weeks of this letter. Father Tucker did go to Wilmington, Delaware, to be with Ed's family. He received this letter from Prince Rainier dated 12 February 61.

Dear Father:

Grace and I learned the very sad news of the death of your brother by a phone call from Monaco.

And we want you to know that all our most affectionate and grieved thoughts are with you in these cruel and "hurting" moments.

Please, Father dear, accept our warmest sympathy and all your very affectionate feelings towards you and those you love.

Can there be any consolation that even these heartbreaking events are of the formal will of God. And that it is He who knows so much better than we poor mortals what is the value of life, its meaning and when "time is up" for each of us.

It is certainly harder for those who remain than for those who depart! We stay to regret — and to cry the departure of those we dearly loved.

But you must know and feel that you have in Monaco and in the Palace a family of yours and that there is around you and for you a lot of affection and love.

God is perfectly good and generous and I am sure that He is very fond of you!

Again, dear Father, all our deepest sympathy and all our affection.

Very sincerely,
Rainier

What can be added to that beautiful letter. In the spring of 1961, Father Tucker made a visit to the United States that included a visit to Hollywood. He spent a few days in Santa Barbara where Joe and Edna

175

had come to be with their son, Joseph, during Mary's illness. He presided at grandnephew Gregory's First Communion, a family coup.

April 18, 1961

Dear Doctor Joe:

My return here has been hectic, as you may imagine, due to a ten-week absence and the accumulation of unfinished business and clients from Princes, Bishops, Oblates, Government people down to the usual parade of commoners, pests, and other pious people.

Your Mother's Easter greetings brought me hopeful news of Mary who is each day at the altar in my humble supplications. The Princess inquires for her assiduously.

The Second Graders of Mt. Carmel School sent me a fine letter telling me that my request for prayers for RAIN had to wait but three days, till the 15th, to be granted! ... the latter bearing among a whole lot of signatures, that of one KEVIN TUCKER.

Albert wants to know if KEVIN will take my place as priest of the palace if I ever die?

I did so enjoy my visit to Santa Barbara, and can never forget Father Cook's wonderful hospitality and fraternal consideration. PLEASE tell him so till I can catch up to my desk-work.

Has Grandpop had any more trouble with his breathing apparatus, and liquids and so on, since my departure? I was sure glad he and the Queen-Mother were not with me on the PAN AM flying from NY to NICE. A hydraulic-brake sprung a leak, causing us to circle over Barcelona for more than an hour to lose speed and weight before landing, and causing also the scare of our lives. We knew we were in danger; fire-engines and ambulances awaiting us at the field! But the pilot made it, helped by our prayers, as never before.

Thank the Queen-Mother for the goose-egg she sent me at Easter. I loved it and the card saying that it brought good wishes "EVEN THOUGH I AM A BROTHER!"

LOVE and blessing to all, and let's have some NEWS.
JFT

✦✦✦

June 16, 1961

Dear Joe:
Through all this wonderful experience I'm made to appreciate and esteem our origin and the blood that is in us. I'm a priest of the DeValeras — saying Mass for them daily and living their life with them. Proud to be a Hickey-Tucker!

Love to all!
JFT

A visit to Ireland with the Prince and Princess. Life at the top and a slight touch of Irish chauvinism.

29 July '61

My dear brother Daddy:
It must be edifying to the faithful and to non-believers as well as puzzling to obstetricians to see you and Edna with the latest edition of your own flesh-and-blood come to life around you.

Of course, the world knows that I have made hurried-up mystery trips to places far off, with unwed and wedded refugees from scandal-mongers and innocents abroad.

It was a relief for me to learn that the Canasta girls had taken back my sister-in-law, as a card from Atlantic City assured me.

Needless to say, I am proud of what you are doing to Stephen who is, after all, my grandnephew, if not my nephew! May God bless and reward you for it and grant you years to see him grow and wax strong in wisdom and grace before God and men. I hope to see him in October.

I have absolutely refused and still do refuse to accept any nomination at the Chapter of Assisi. I am all for ANY American the Europeans will agree on, just so the present administration is swept out. That's one reason I declare myself out of the running, if only to force others out. I know that the Americans and the Europeans want me to accept. I cannot honestly do it, physically, mentally, financially, or religiously. Not that Monaco is the reason! But HOME is! I want to be free to be with you all when you need me, and as the occasion requires. Whoever is elected, you'll know that he was MY choice.

Love to all,
JFT

Joe and Edna nurtured their infant grandson, Stephen, at their home in Wilmington, Delaware, for several months until the return to health of his mother, Mary, that occurred in September 1961.

Once again Father Francis talks emphatically about his refusal to become the Superior General of his religious order and his determination to clean house at its top.

"HOME" emphasized again. Not so much being there as being able to be there.

29 August, 1961

Dear Joe:
The "HOME-news" your letter from the Cameo Cocktail Lounge of the Drake Wiltshire overlooking Union Square in San Francisco, came to me via Wilmington (which might mean that I am guilty of harboring stolen goods — to wit, the letter),

and while I share in good Doctor Joe's distress, I also thank God that he is favored by his and Mary's families in the providential help afforded him through them. It is all quite natural, after all, isn't it, and for our side, it's running true to form — Grandpop Hickey rescuing Mother and her brood — when things were tough, but so was he!

... I plan to have my Jubilee Mass at Saint Peter's shortly after arrival, by arrangement with Monsignor Sweeney and Frank Dougherty at Sallies. If Saint Anthony's wants to stage a parish celebration for me afterwards, O.K., but I want it understood that my fiftieth is not their party, as was the 25th. (You remember: no purse! They handed me a bag of change supposed to be the collection at the mass — charged 5 bucks for a dollar-and-a-half meal, and applied the surplus to themselves).

The 10th, I had a quiet low mass in the private chapel of the Prince's summer home, with none but Rainier and Grace and Caroline and Albert and Grand-pop Pierre and the five Oblates that are with me here. 'Twas just what I wanted, like at my Ordination — no one but Tom Lawless, Bill McLaughlin and a couple of the local confreres.

At Ed's death, the Prince wrote me: "Remember, you have another family over here," and I'm sure you'll agree that's pretty decent, because he meant it, and they do, all of them, show me reverence as well as affection.

And this brings me to correct your impression, Joe, that it is on account of them that I refused the Generalship. That's not the case at all. Rainier was ready to do all he could to help me get the job IF I wanted it. I absolutely did not want it — I did want to prevent Balducelli's re-election. And he would have had it, IF I didn't spring the "old-age" gag, including the enclosure which shows that NO Superior General, not even Father Brisson, was OVER 70 when elected. It's O.K. for a

*Pope to take his job at 78. BUT they carry him around in a
chair! The Superior General MUST visit ALL and every house
of the Institute every 3 years — my trip to Africa was enough
for me, and I only half did it at that. The same trip KILLED
Father Lebeau and unseated him in 4 years, as the diagram
shows. Father Berther, the one you met with me at Albano, was
paralyzed before his 12 years were up. Then, Joe, Balducelli is
leaving things in such a mess that, NO THANKS — there's
sure no honor in cleaning it up. I wanted an American, NO
MATTER WHO! ... I hope that neither you nor he think that at
this late age I've gone completely off! I know what I'm doing,
for the Oblates, for myself and Family, including the Lady in
Heaven (who surely agrees), and for the Church of God — I
can't quit the post I'm at without the Vatican's permission.
Two Popes asked me to stay on, and Cardinal Tardini, before
dying, reminded me of this, as does his successor, Archbishop
Samore, as great a friend of mine as was Tardini. I do have
diplomatic standing at the Vatican, you know.*

*Every Legation in Rome knows that and so do the Bishops
of France and the world over. These gentlemen never knew
there was an Oblate Superior General in existence, nor most of
them Oblates at all (except the few Bishops where they worked)
till Tardini appointed me first for ten years (1950 to 1960, and
then RENEWED the appointment for another ten years — to
1970).*

*This renewal was an outstanding favor bringing with it
prestige and respect for therecipient.*

*At Cardinal Tardini's funeral, I was with his family at the
ceremonies in Saint Peter's. He left me a set of silver
candelabra he used at Mass. I was among the prelates who
offered Mass in the Vatican all 3 days that his remains were
there. Now, no Superior General got to do that.*

Had I become Superior General, I should have been

*compelled to give up my place in Vatican ranks, and one is not
expected to do that unless he be the indispensable man, and I
really am not that. If I had done that, Joe, the headlines in the
papers over here would herald: "PERE TUCKER, FALLEN
INTO DISGRACE" — "PERE TUCKER, KICKED UP-
STAIRS" — "TUCKER DIES WITH TARDINI" —
"OBLATES TAKE HIM TO SAVE HIM" — and I am not
exaggerating a bit.*

*I was the youngest of the Council. When I claimed the age
excuse, the others HAD to and all four went out, leaving the
succession to younger men. Adenauer and De Gaulle are as
gaga as Winnie Churchill and Mamie Eisenhower's husband!
It's not every oldster who can rejuvenate to second parenthood
at your age. The rule is to fall into second childhood. And most
of us do, except the very wise ones who KNOW when their time
is up!*

*So, cheerio, Joe, quite a difference between the job that's
too big for the man — and the man who is too big for the job!*

Love to all — let's hear from you!

JFT

Father Tucker was returning to Wilmington to celebrate the 50th anniversary of his ordination to the priesthood. The actual anniversary
date, 10 August 1961, he celebrated with the Royal Family, as he says.

He really "opens up" in his detailed exploration of his refusal
of the Generalship. Strategy, tactic and results. Evidently, he expected
his brother Joe to pass the word to his many supporters who did not
understand his decision. Basically, he was saying that their view of
him was too provincial.

Sept. 25, 1961

Dear Joe:
At last all the Okays needed for date of departure and length of

stay are in hand. Those to wit of our new Father General, the Prince, and the Bishop!

Sunday, Oct. 1st, Saint Charles' parish is staging its celebration of the event of half-a-century, Masses and General Communion all day (kids just got back from vacation), the Prince and Princess will attend the 11 o'clock mass, and Father General will be on hand, and so on. The parish is giving me a 6-foot carved wood statue of Saint Francis de Sales with a memorial marble slab "To their Reverend Pastor, JOHN FRANCIS TUCKER, OSFS, the parish in grateful homage on the occasion of his GOLDEN JUBILEE in the priesthood: 1911–1961."

About our family, I thought it might be nice for me, on the day you choose, to celebrate mass in the Cemetery chapel and visit our heavenly jubilee-girls and boys from the fourth generation back. And then for the living who hunger and thirst for justice, have them quenched and filled as and where you see fit. ... Why not restrict that party to adults andhave another party for the children, where they'll suffer no danger of being disappointed, shocked, or scandalized by those of Jubilee age?

Happily, I chose all my relatives, even binding most of them in the indissoluble ties of wedlock and making of their offspring heirs of the Kingdom of Tuck! and GOD!

Love to all!

JFT

Father Tucker stayed in the United States over 2 months on this visit. During his stay, he began arranging his permanent return to the USA.

The following is an article from *The Journal – Every Evening* (Wilmington, Delaware) dated November 13, 1961:

The Next 50 Years —
Banquet Honors Father Tucker

The Very Reverend Canon J. Francis Tucker revealed his plans "for the next 50 years" at a banquet honoring his 50th Anniversary in the Catholic priesthood yesterday.

Father Tucker, chaplain to the royal family of Monaco, said he will continue in the capacity.

He recalled that when the late Pope Pius XII met Prince Rainier and Princess Grace, he told Father Tucker "Stay with them."

FATHER TUCKER, the first American to be ordained in the order of the Oblates of Saint Francis de Sales, is the order's first American to reach his golden jubilee. He was ordained Aug. 10, 1911, in Rome.

Among the congratulatory messages read at the banquet in Salesianum School was one from Pope John XXIII, conveyed in a telegram from the papal secretary of state, Amleto Cardinal Cicognani.

Others came from Francis Cardinal Spellman of New York, Eamon de Valera, president of Ireland, and a number of officials and prelates from all parts of the world.

AMONG THEM also was one which closed with "Don't forget to come home." It was signed "Rainier and Grace," reminder to the audience of 900 in the Salesianum gymnasium that Father Tucker is still chaplain to the royal family of Monaco. Princess Grace's mother, Mrs. John B. Kelly of Philadelphia, attended the mass and sat next to Father Tucker at the banquet.

Father Tucker celebrated Mass yesterday in Saint Anthony's Church, the church he founded. The Most Reverend Dr. Michael W. Hyle, bishop of Wilmington, presided in the sanctuary.

Bishop Hyle, who spoke at the banquet after the Mass, said Father Tucker has earned and kept the affection in which he is held.

A SECOND speaker, the Very Reverend John J. Conmy, provincial superior of the Oblates in North America, noting the growth of the order to its 600 plus, said, "certainly the seed he has planted has brought forth a harvest."

The Right Reverend Monsignor James M. Grant, pastor of Saint Elizabeth's Church, also celebrating his 50th year in the priesthood, also spoke. The Very Reverend William A. Stahl, assistant provincial, presented a purse to Father Tucker on behalf of friends.

The purse contained $50 for each of Father Tucker's 50 years in the priesthood, whichFather Stahl said "we give you — as a starter."

The toastmaster, the Very Reverend John F. Tocik, the Oblates' director of education, listed some of the "firsts" of Father Tucker: First Salesianum student, first American Oblate, first American provincial, first pastor of Saint Anthony's, first American member of the Oblates general council, first Oblate chaplain to the royal family of Monaco.

BRINGING greetings from the state with brief remarks at the banquet were U.S. Sen. J. Caleb Boggs, Mayor John E. Babiarz and State Sen. John E. Reilly, representing Gov. Elbert N. Carvel. Various members of the state, city and county agencies, the General Assembly and the judiciary were spotted throughout the room.

The Right Reverend Monsignor Joseph D. Sweeney, Vicar General of the Wilmington diocese, delivered the sermon at the jubilee mass.

◆◆◆

Jan 29, 1962

Dear Joe:
All of a week that I'm here, safe but not too sound because of
that bad cold I brought with me from the USA. It's stubborn
even against the horrible remedies they're injecting into me
from all quarters and positions. Takes time, is all the MDs tell
me. Trip was fine. Fathers Boston and Tom at port to bring me
to Monaco. Prince and Princess both hugged me — tough to
take in public! The Bishop, too, embraced me. Tell Phyllis and
Mary if they think their old Uncle is a kisser, they ought to see
him in royal action. I phoned Rome, to Father Bill, and shall
go to see him as soon as the Grimaldis get off to Switzerland. I
said Caroline's 5-year-old Birthday Mass in the palace. More
kissing — although Albert treats me a bit like Steve! Hope
Edna is beering it up! LOVE to all, including Frankie Pan.
Let friends know you heard from me.
    Cheerio!
    JFT

His annual flu! And more affection from the royal family.

Feb. 18, 1962

Dear Joe:
So Happy to hear that the Queen-Mother Edna is able to
preside, as usual, at home-affairs, and to hold court for the
Canasta ladies.
    Prince Pierre came back from American Hospital in Paris
yesterday — not much improved, nor shall he ever be. I am to
go see him tomorrow.
    My part of the royal family is still in Switzerland with
Father Jimmie Boston, skiing when not saying Mass! Father

*Tom O'Connell, a Swiss Oblate, and an Italian are with me
and all is going well. I am very happy about my return here
and happier, still, that it will come to an honorable end in
June. The politicians had plotted to sink me with Rainier in the
debacle with the French Government, about which I sent you a
news account. Cardinal Cicognani told me to "stay put" and
then of my own choice, to shake the dust and dirt of this sunny
spot for shady people, that I have borne for 12 years off my
American-made shoes that Ace Taylor paid for.*

*I am longing to be with you all. Cheerio! Love to great and
small! Enclosure for Edna's Spring bonnet and your own
Bermuda shorts.*

JFT

In early 1962, there was a showdown between De Gaulle and Rainier
over the Principality's tax-exempt status for the citizens of France living there. Rainier "stood tall," but had to change Monaco's taxation
policy for citizens of France. To keep the support of the Monagasques,
he agreed to a new Constitution that reduced, to some extent, his authority in constitutional matters. A secondary theme in this "debacle"
was De Gaulle's displeasure with "American influences" in Monaco.
On this issue Prince Rainier did not back down, but De Gaulle's message was absorbed by the Prince's chaplain.

March 9, 1962

Dear Joe:

*... Things are NOT so bad as printed. They are even good in a
way, I think, and the result will ultimately teach the jealous
stuck-up little Monagasques who want to share in Rainier's
reign, how happier they were when he ran it alone and the
French, how stupid they are to spite their own face by not
biting off Charlie's nose!*

To the staid royalist snobs who claim that "Princesses just

*don't do what Grace is doing" — my standard reply is "And
thank GOD, Grace is not doing what Princesses over here
do!" I say that she is coming back to the USA to get a breath of
clean air. And her husband wants her to. As for me, I announced in January that I wanted to come Home. By so doing,
I am not breaking the ties that bind me to Monaco, anymore
than did I break the ties that bind me to my Homeland when I
came over here. Proof is: I'm coming back!*

   Cheerio!
   JFT

His mention of the De Gaulle affair points up his unwavering loyalty
to the Prince.

Evidently, he knew that Princess Grace was to visit the United States
but did not know why. He was unprepared for the announcement from
the Palace on March 19, 1962 that Princess Grace would return to Hollywood to make a movie under Alfred Hitchcock's direction.

March 26, 1962

Dear Joe:
*The COPIES enclosed will reveal my reaction. They are NOT
for publication, except verbally to such persons as you judge
fit.*

   I got your clippings twice, and thank you for them.
   *The Italian word in my letter to Archbishop O'Connor
means "rift in marital relation."*

   *I have never seen Grace and Rainier more loving and
devoted to one another than they are now. Of course, the
SNOBS, such as Edna's dear old friend, Pierre de Polignac,
andCo., are shocked.*

   *And all the while, what ANTOINETTE, your daughter
Betty's friend, is performing in "REAL" not "reel" life is
perfectly acceptable!*

Shall be GLAD to get HOME!
However, I can't leave during these two crises.
  Love to all,
  JFT

Late in 1982, the writer, shocked by the death of Princess Grace, was prompted to write a book about Grace, Rainier, and Canon Tucker. However, the spate of books about Princess Grace led him to discontinue that project and to wait until the "dust had settled" before writing a book focused on Canon Tucker. Several chapters written early in 1983 have been included in this work. Chapter XV is one of them.

It centers on the "Marnie" affair and its effect upon Princess Grace. The "COPIES enclosed" with the letter of March 26, 1962 are included in it. Chapter XV includes a fictional dialogue between the Prince and chaplain about the Princess.

— 15 —
Hollywood Tomorrow - 1962

Grace Kelly was Hollywood's own, so Hollywood thought, "She will be back." But when? For 6 years, Metro Goldwyn Mayer waited, watched, and enticed as the top female box office attraction of 1955 settled in as Princess, growing in fame and popularity all the while. After all, Prince Rainier had made the decision that Grace would make no more movies. She had seemingly agreed. But all who knew Grace were sure that ultimately she would make the decision. The MGM executives could attest that she had her own way of having her own way.

Many Hollywood creations, male and female stars, of that pre-television day of motion picture chauvinism became so identified with the industry that they thought of themselves as an "in group" with a common "motion picture" identity. They could not conceive that Grace Kelly was not one of them. In an episode in Kitty Kelly's biography, "Elizabeth Taylor, The Last Star," she tells of the lavish 40th birthday party arranged for Elizabeth by Richard Burton at Budapest, Hungary to which Princess Grace and Prince Rainier were invited.

Elizabeth instructed the designer to redecorate some of the hotel suites for the most important guests, such as Princess Grace. She even arranged for him to visit various homes throughout Budapest to borrow the antiques and paintings he would need.

"We can't move out of our suite because it would take weeks to get my things out of there, so make a Royal one for Grace," said Elizabeth. "Make it pretty enough for a Princess, Larry, but remember, she's just like us."

Though this happened years after the events of 1962, it shows an "in group" view of their Grace Kelly. Little wonder that many of them thought that Princess Grace would return. For them, an acting career was first choice, above which there could be no higher choice.

"The Kelly Family" biographer, John McCollum, in 1956 wrote wisely about Grace Kelly's triumph in her award for Best Actress of the Year in 1954 for "The Country Girl."

Reaching this night, the biggest night in an actress' career, had been no easy path for Grace. If the public only knew what she had endured to get there — so many hours posing for countless publicity stills, indoor and out, spending hours in a darkened theater auditioning, and eagerly hearing others read their parts, modeling and taking bit parts until The Break came along. Those long hours of waiting outside the casting office, hoping terribly that she got the part — any part — wanting it so much, and frightened to death that she wouldn't get it. Strange how this world, the world of theater, grabbed and held you and wouldn't let go. Indeed, there was only one life for an actress — the life of the theater. It was like a contagious fever. But Grace wouldn't have it any other way. She had made the grade, her name was in lights — the Actress of the Year — and there was no reward to compare.

Maurice Zolotow, a perceptive, supportive motion picture industry friend of Grace Kelly wrote in *The American Weekly* at the time of her marriage:

As a detached and sympathetic observer of the psychological conflicts and the intense struggles which Grace Kelly has experienced in order to carve out her great achievement as an actress, I do not believe that she can be happy unless she continues to do the work that has come to represent for her the special and private fulfillment of all her creative desires. Acting got Grace Kelly, symbolizes the solid ground on which she stands with her own two feet. It represents her triumph as a human being, her victory over all the doubts and insecurities that have haunted her life since childhood. To turn her back on all this, I believe, would be a terrible defeat for her. It would be like cutting the heart out of herself.

The insightful views of McCollum and Zolotow add depth to Elizabeth Taylor's, "Remember, she's just like us." It was a compliment, that of one fine artist for another. And an intuitive recognition of the power of the theater.

Several movies were planned for Grace Kelly at the time of her engagement and wedding. "High Society" was filmed just prior to her marriage, and she herself had said that she might make one more movie, "Designing Women," for MGM following her honeymoon to fulfill a contractual obligation to that studio. But the Prince and she resolved that potential conflict neatly by starting a family immediately. Besides, as we have seen, she had the most demanding role of her life to learn in that palace in Monaco. So MGM thought that it had a "rain check." Though the studio had eventually lifted its suspension (Grace Kelly may hold the record for longest suspension of a female star by a major studio), it obtained a first option on any commercial film she might make. Consequently, MGM "tracked" Princess Grace's movements, particularly when she came to the United States. Hollywood was ready, if ...

Rumors that Princess Grace would resume her movie career began at her wedding and reappeared frequently. The rumor that she would return to Hollywood soon after the birth of her second child prompted Prince Rainier to check its sources. Hollywood, as he suspected. MCA, the Princess' agents, continued to send her scripts, which she reviewed diligently. With Prince Rainier's complete support, she maintained her friendships with many of her movie industry associates. Indeed, many became close friends of the Prince as well.

By 1961, Grace Kelly had become Princess Grace in the world's view. The Monacoans loved her and were sure she loved them in return. For this "Princess" was not just a word and images. She performed and everyone knew it. In five short, wonderful years, a strong, happy, determined husband, two beautiful children, a new tourism, a changing image for Monaco, real changes for the ill, aged, and underprivileged. Charisma! All Monaco felt it. Indescribable! One had to feel it.

A shy, introspective Princess Grace knew she was doing well. Her unique Grace Kelly style was surviving. Her personal discipline, professional training, and life values were working for her as before. Now, she was unique among princesses as she had been unique among actresses. Her dedication to a position she had freely accepted was complete. She wanted no other. But, now that she had mastered it, could she not take a vacation from it for a few short months? Her vacation doing what she wanted to do? Suddenly, she was vulnerable. And Hollywood struck.

Alfred Hitchcock had been mentor, sponsor, and friend to Grace Kelly. His recognition of her talent and her appeal, along with his keen sense as to how to develop both, made Grace Kelly a Star. Their relationship was one of trust, that of true friends. Sensing that Grace might be ready and seeing no harm coming to her in making another movie, he approached her directly in late 1961 about appearing as the lead in "Marnie," another thriller. Princess Grace was intrigued. She saw that her fee, which would approach a million dollars or more, could be directed towards a children's charity in Monaco which she sponsored. As Gwen Robyns, Princess Grace's biographer, so succinctly describes, the Princess let Hitchcock do the persuading.

When the final commitment had to be made, Mr. Hitchcock himself went to Monaco. With great tact, Princess Grace let the producer tell Prince Rainier about his plans, as she knew that he was a man of tremendous discretion, wisdom, and selling power.

It may also have been a much more womanly wile in that she was making it easier for Prince Rainier to say no to Hitchcock rather than to her. Everyone, including Prince Rainier, knew how much she longed to make this film.

After she had decided, Grace let the men decide. On May 19, 1962 a formal announcement from the Palace stated:

A spokesman for the Prince of Monaco announced today that Princess Grace has accepted to appear during her summer vacation in a motion picture for Mister Alfred Hitchcock to be made in the United States. The Princess has previously starred in three films for Mister Hitchcock, Dial M for Murder, Rear Window and To Catch a Thief. The film, to start in late summer, is based on a suspense novel by the English writer Winston Graham. It is understood that Prince Rainier will most likely be present during part of the film making depending on his schedule, and that Princess Grace will return to Monaco by the beginning of November.

That there might be some criticism of this decision must have been foreseen, but the wave of universal disbelief and displeasure was a shock to Princess, Prince, and Hitchcock. The entire Riviera reacted with disbelief. But none more so than the residents of Monaco, particularly the Monagasques. They were horrified and in despair. The working and middle class citizens of Monaco and its environs had developed an attachment to Princess Grace that could not have been realized until this threat that "she is leaving" arose. A dozen or more years later, Gwen Robyns recalls a conversation with a Monagasque cab driver.

"Is good princess," he said. "The first year we did not know if Hollywood princess or real princess. Now we know she is real princess. But she is more than that. She is good mother and she lives her religion. That is more important than being princess. We are all family people and we know she has to be in Paris to be with daughter Caroline and to visit her mother in America. But it is not the same when she is not here. Princess Grace belongs to us and we belong to her."

Who could say it better? Princess Grace was family. And "family" she already was by 1961, only 5 years after coming to Monaco. This fact belies a contention that the Monagasque's dismay at the announcement of her return to Hollywood was prompted only by their own self-interest. They were also concerned for the Princess. What would happen to her? As Prince Rainier had said, many Monagasques of that time had in their lifetimes traveled little more than 20 miles from the Principality. Television was new to them; they saw few motion pictures. Their views of actors, actresses, and entertainers was jaundiced at best. And, God knows, since the coming of the casino in the 1860's they and their ancestors had been able to witness first-hand extravagances and decadence at its ultimate among the privileged — with Russian nobility leading the way. This Royal Family, as elegant as any, was seemingly so different. What was happening?

As family, they felt rejected. They had no warning. Security turned to fear. What about the future? Would France take over? Would Princess Grace spend little time in Monaco? Was she less committed to her marriage and her status as Princess than they thought? Did she wish to return to the United States and not be a citizen of Monaco? Was she really unhappy, as some had said? And, so it went! Speculation turned to accusation for some. Unkind words were spoken and circulated. They were amazed, shocked, disappointed, disillusioned. Their vision of a prosperous, happy future was shattered, so insecure were the incident-battered Monagasques.

The High Society habitués of the Riviera were taken completely by surprise. The gossip experts of the Western World had nothing to prepare them for the Palace's announcement. Except for a cherished group of close friends, princely relatives, and business associates, Prince and Princess remained aloof from the coteries of royalty, ex-royalty, new and old rich, and social aspirants that preserved the shady reputation of the Riviera. Both refused to be the leaders of a vacuous, party-going Riviera society. Both detested snobs and social climbers; very few managed to get beyond the Palace gates. To associate with Princess Grace, one joined in her charitable and beautification projects — Red Cross, gardens, hospitals, nursing homes — but not at high visibility parties, of which both Prince and Princess had their share officially.

Tongues wagged. The absence of facts perfected the gossip. They had been saying she wasn't a real princess all along. She had avoided them to keep from being discovered. This last criticism aroused Father Tucker and prompted him to say:

To the said royalist snobs who claim that "Princesses just don't do what Grace is doing" — my standard reply is "And thank God, Grace is not doing what princesses over here do!" I say she is coming back to the USA to get a breath of clean air. And her husband wants her to.

Father Tucker's opinion of Riviera high society was one-to-one with that of Prince and Princess.

But there were the trusted friends, relatives, and associates, too, who were dismayed. Even Prince Pierre, the Prince's father, who loved, advised, and supported Princess Grace, had not been consulted. Terminally ill, Prince Pierre emphatically expressed his disapproval to Prince Rainier. With more need for tact, others discreetly expressed their concern to the Prince through those who were "his eyes and ears" to the world. The onerous task of reporting to Prince and Princess the adverse reactions, seemingly of everyone, fell to George Lukomski, a key member of the Palace staff and trusted friend of the Royal couple. Mr. Lukomski, in turn, was shaken by the horror and grief with which Grace and Rainier received the deluge of criticism of what was a family decision about a summer vacation that would provide a much-needed diversion for the Princess while benefiting the underprivileged of Monaco.

There is nothing more ephemeral than "good relations with the Press." In the Western World, the Free Press feels dulled by a continuing cozy relationship with government, politician, or celebrity. It eschews goodwill and objectivity passionately and is sentimental only about itself. Prince Rainier had many a bruise from the gossip columnist Free Press (free trip, free lodgings, free lunch, free . . .) and had learned the hard way to improve his handling of it but, in this case, "took his eye off the ball." The Press had no warning before the announcement and got a couple of days of "no comment" afterward.

In all fairness, the collective Press, both the responsible and the salacious, was treated ineptly. It was unreasonable to believe that the Press could accept the formal Palace Announcement without asking "Why?" And there was no answer in Monaco as to why known to any other than Prince, Princess, and, possibly, Alfred Hitchcock. The Press went to work to find out "Why" one way or another. The American Press got this from Mr. Hitchcock:

Petaluma (California) — Princess Grace will receive the immense sum of one million dollars for her interpretation of the title role in the film "Marnie," which she will make under the direction of Mr. Alfred Hitchcock. To this figure will be added the box-office percentages. Mr. Hitchcock gave this detail to the press in Petaluma, where he is at present making the film, "The Birds." Mr. Hitchcock also specifies that it was after reading the story that Princess Grace offered to play the title role. She has recently announced that she will donate the profits from the film to a children's home, which she intends founding in Monaco.

A few "why's" were being answered — an attractive role and a major charitable project — but surely there was more to it than that. The French Press intimated that there had been a "rift in marital relation," a claim that led Canon Tucker to write, "I have never seen Grace and Rainier more loving and devoted to one another than they are now. Of course the SNOBS ... are shocked."

Other very damaging speculation included: "She is a princess actress rather than actress princess;" "Princess Grace is tired and bored in her role as a Princess and wants to leave Monaco, at least temporarily;" "Wearied by infighting with the National Council and his struggle with the French government, Prince Rainier is preparing to leave;" "For health reasons, the Princess prefers not to live in Monaco." And there was much more. When the Press has no lines to read between, it will read between its own. As Canon Tucker once wrote: "The Press had to have its innings — that's how they make their living. But, thank God, I weathered the storm." Prince and Princess were suddenly caught in a maelstrom that continued to intensify, and they had to weather it alone.

The Church was caught off guard. Both the Vatican and the Diocese of Monaco had no forewarning of the announcement. Neither Canon Tucker nor any other clergy close to the Royal Couple were aware of the negotiations with Hitchcock or of the terse announcement. The Vatican was very concerned at the implications of the decision and the damage to the reputations of the Royal Couple by the unseemly clamor of the World Press. Years of positive, visible exposition of Catholic family and social values were about to be irretrievably lost.

Monaco, a last remnant of the Holy Roman Empire and a Roman Catholic enclave, had become, under Prince Rainier, a visible exemplar of Rome's exposition of Catholic doctrine and philosophy in its worship, its social programs and family living. Prince and Princess were responsible, not capricious. And then, suddenly, the announcement.

The Church never doubted either Prince's or Princess' personal integrity in this matter. The issues lay in symbols and values. The Roman Catholic Church understands the meaning of the Symbolic Act as does no other organization. It understands the conflict between being a private person and a public figure. It understands and does not underestimate the sacrifices a public figure must make in the private person. The deeds and behavior of a public figure in public can be symbolic acts reflective of social standards and values in spite of the personal private imperfections of the public figure. A public figure simply cannot be a private person in a public arena. A shy, humble, lovely Princess Grace was seeking to be a private person in a most public place — Hollywood. Impossible!

At best, the Vatican would consider Hollywood an amoral force that could on occasion be put to good use. Co-existence is possible, at least temporarily. The Vatican's concern was that now that Grace Kelly, an exemplary professional actress, had grown to become an even more exemplary Princess — a model of motherhood and social leadership — the super imposition of a public image as Princess with the public image of actress would demean the former. The public would see on the screen a person it now knew as Princess Grace as Marnie, a charming but professional thief. The "Symbolic Act" was likely to be the message that one can be a success in either role by being a clever actress without depth of character being required for either. Though untrue, and unfair to the private Grace, that message was likely to be conveyed and she would have a difficult time becoming a credible Princess Grace again in a world view, even though Monagasques might be placated.

For the Church, the Announcement was not simply a public relations gaffe. The return of Princess Grace to a commercial Hollywood would be the wrong Symbolic Act, no matter how well her decision was rationalized or protestations about her true interests were promulgated — true though they certainly would be. Princess Grace could no more return to the commercial theater than Prince Rainier could become manager of the Casino. The Grimaldis had maintained a high measure of credibility by distancing themselves from that phenomenon from its beginning. And yet, as Canon Tucker points out, Prince and Princess, as private partners, had arrived at an honest, courageous, thoroughly Christian decision. Gallic irony, indeed.

The chaplain was surprised. He was not even among the small group

197

of Palace insiders to whom Princess Grace had personally announced her decision. But an insider he was; very close to Prince and Princess, affectionately esteemed by them both. Yet for this crucial decision he was not consulted, perhaps because they were certain what his counsel would be.

With the coming of Grace Kelly to Monaco, Canon Tucker adopted a low-key, low visibility stance, preferring to live and work behind the scenes, yet to be privy to the most intimate concerns of the Principality. In 1958, he is quoted as saying, "I believe the Princess has received offers to appear in films and plays. But I don't think she will ever go back to the cinema. If she asks me, I would certainly advise against it." And, on another occasion, "Grace go back to films? Nonsense. They couldn't offer her a role in Hollywood as good as the one she is playing now."

What, then, had happened to the sensitive "antenna" by which he could so often figure "two and two" from small clues? He had gotten no clues. Actually, Father Tucker had beenaway from Monaco during the time that Hitchcock had contacted Princess Grace. During his 4-month stay in the United States, he had formally celebrated the anniversary of his 50th year as an Oblate of Saint Francis de Sales and made preliminary arrangements to return to the United States for good. In his 73rd year, he was finding the "grind" in Monaco a bit more than he wished to cope with. But he had been warmly welcomed back to Monaco. On January 29, 1962, he wrote to a relative in his best "hunt and peck" style:

All of a week that I'm here, safe but not too sound because of that bad cold I brought with me from USA. It's stubborn even against the horrible remedies they're injecting into me from all quarters and positions. Takes time, is all the MDs tell me. Trip was fine. Fathers Boston and Tom at port to bring me to Monaco. Prince and Princess both hugged me — tough to take in public! The Bishop, too, embraced me. Tell Phyllis and Mary if they think their old Uncle is a kisser, they ought to see him in royal action. I phoned to Rome to Father Bill, and shall go to see him as soon as the Grimaldis get off to Switzerland. I said Caroline's 5-year-old Birthday Mass in the palace. More kissing — although Albert treats me a bit like Steve!

On his return, Canon Tucker was preoccupied catching up with his "desk." And then the Grimaldis were off to Switzerland for a winter vacation. He had very limited contact with them during the 6 months prior to the Announcement. His reaction is best stated in his own words in two personal, closely guarded, previously unpublished letters, one to Prince Rainier on March 20, 1962, the day following the Announcement, the second to Archbishop O'Connor at the Vatican on March 25, 1962.

March 20, 1962

My dear Lord Prince:
I am very proud of You, very grateful to You for the news released from the Palace yesterday.

A wonderful, generous, noble gesture towards Your wife and Her people.

A courageous rebuke to Old World snobbism and pietistic hypocrisy.

A timely, Providential offensive in defense of Your personal and sovereign rights.

A brave Declaration of Independence.

A correct Catholic position in relation to what is right and what is wrong according to Divine standards as opposed to human prejudices.

I am the more grateful to Your Highness for sparing me any and all direct intervention in the decision that might have provoked upon me an increase of scorn and contempt from the unmerciful.

Won't You share with the dear Princess all these thoughts of mine and assure me that both of You will always share with me mutual abiding affection and loyalty!

JFT

✦✦✦

March 25, 1962

My dear Archbishop,
I feel it incumbent upon me to acquaint Your Excellency by
way of information with the recent news released from the
Palace of Monaco in date of March 19th.
It is absolutely false that there has been or is what the press
calls "disappori conjugali" between Rainier and Grace.
The decision about the Cinema was taken during my
absence in America for my sacerdotal fiftieth anniversary,
extending from Oct. 1st, 1961 to Jan. 21st, 1962.
The decision was not revealed to me till the official publi-
cation, March 19th. I then learned from the Prince that it was a
joint decision taken in family council, and considered by them
a strictly family affair. I am happy that I was not brought into
it.
In face of the "fait accompli," and in possession of the
knowledge the Prince has given me of his reasons for the
decision, I can but agree with those reasons and stand by to
help Rainier and Grace in the religious domain "ad nutum
Superiorum."
I have, of course, submitted this information to the Bishop
of Monaco. Begging Your blessing on a tired and tried old
friend, I still remain,
il poverello di Monte-Carlo,
  JFT

In both of these letters, Canon Tucker separates himself from the
decision-making process. In his letter to Archbishop O'Connor, he indicates that the "fait accompli" left him with the role only of providing
Rainier and Grace the support that a chaplain should give. In his letter
to the Prince, he lists only the reasons why Rainier was correct. Only

by thanking the Prince for not including him in the decision does he indicate that he might have counseled against it.

The statement "A correct Catholic position" may need explanation in light of the Vatican's and his own concern about the decision. Prince Rainier had supported a personal legitimate concern of his wife in her best interest. At a family level, he was correct. He put aside concerns about his personal image, royal prejudices, possible political implications, and so on. He made a "selfless decision in the best interest of another." "A Good Samaritan" decision, a correct Catholic position. The existential implications of the decision were overlooked. Two shy, sensitive, intelligent, self-effacing lovers like Rainier and Grace just could not take themselves that seriously. Someone would have to tell them. Their chaplain knew that. He alone could have, but ...

For Prince Rainier III of Monaco, 1962 was a pivotal year. As the year began, he was locked in a parliamentary struggle with the National Council. Onassis and he were close to the breaking point over the policies of the Societe des Bains de Mer that controlled the Casino, and he had reached an impasse with France over Monaco's economic development policies and tax exempt status of French nationals living in Monaco. The latter alone threatened the sovereignty of the principality. And accompanying it was the observation that the Prince's affinity for advice from his American economic advisor, Dole, and his American chaplain, Canon Tucker, showed him to be less pro-France than the super nationalist Charles De Gaulle would desire.

The Prince was also disturbed by the serious illness of his father, Prince Pierre, and by Canon Tucker's expressed intention to return permanently to the United States. His one consolation amid these travails was living with Princess Grace and his children and his great pride at Princess Grace's accomplishments with the Monagasque community. And then Mr. Alfred Hitchcock came to dinner.

Hitchcock's reasoned proposal minimized difficulties the Royal Family might have as the Princess acted in the movie "Marnie." It would be made in California during the Princess' 2-month vacation; secluded, attractive housing would be provided for the Prince, Princess, and children; the proceeds to the Princess would be distributed as she should choose. These accommodations removed a potential "family" argument against the proposal that it would be impractical and inconvenient. Through both the timing and circumstances of his proposal, the astute

Mr. Hitchcock had placed Prince Rainier in a most awkward position.

The Prince had two alternatives:

– argue that the best interests of the principality should have precedence over the best interests of Princess Grace;

– argue that the best interests of Princess Grace should have precedence over the best interests of the principality.

He had to choose between a family decision or a state decision. For a state decision he would surely consult his top advisors. For a family decision they would not necessarily be consulted. He decided it should be a family decision. Why?

At the time of his engagement to Princess Grace, Prince Rainier had said that her duties and status as Princess would not permit continuance of an actress' career. As late as 1958, he had checked on the source of rumors she would return. In 1958, the Princess' secretary announced: "She has told me to say that her film career is definitely finished." Seemingly, Rainier had changed his mind for some reason by early 1962. Actually, he had not. He remained opposed and was certain that Princess Grace was a true artist whose skill and style were aesthetically transforming Monaco. Certainly, a hobby was a family affair. In his considerations, unchecked with others, he saw little threat to the principality from her engaging in a personal hobby that as a by-product would support a Monacoan charity dear to the Princess' heart. Neither did she, obviously.

As Father Tucker wrote: He *"had never seen Grace and Rainier more deeply in love than they were at that moment."* Their family life was idealistic, they were close and unthreatened. But, the Prince noted:

There have been times, you know, when the Princess has been a little melancholic — which I quite understand — about having performed a form of art very successfully only to be cut away from it completely, cut away not only from acting personally but from watching other actors, whom we do not have much occasion to see down here.

So Prince Rainier not only decided to support Princess Grace's vacation project but encouraged her "because I thought it would do her a lot of good." A noble miscalculation! Neither Princess Grace nor he were at that point deeply aware of the public's (not the press') reverence of them as a Royal Couple. The press had taken on the job of keeping them humble by fair means and foul. Possibly, the press had been too successful. The public knew better. It had a profound sense of the quality of this beautiful Princess whom it was getting to know so well since her husband delighted in having her "take center stage" with the public.

Prince Rainier said "yes" and authorized the release of a Palace Announcement. Unfortunately, he did not check the copy before it was released.

Princess Grace was thrilled that a challenging role would be offered her at one of the few times she could be available to take it. Her pure motivation was to develop her craftsmanship as a professional actress. She had worked slavishly to develop her talent and knew, as did many others, that she had not reached her full potential when she "withdrew" at the age of 26. As Gwen Robyns noted, Grace thought her way into her roles. Carefully, she had thought her way into the role of "Marnie." She knew she could meet the challenge of it with Alfred Hitchcock directing. She doubted not at all that, in spite of all the other plums that could go with her return to the movies, his motivation as an artist would be to guide her to reaching new heights as an actress. For two pure artists, all the other considerations were necessary, often annoying fluff, to be tolerated so that they could perform. Grace was euphoric. Nothing could "recharge her batteries" to continue as wife, mother, and princess more that a brief interlude in that cinema world she loved. Crash!

"Grace is devastated, Father, I am worried sick about her."

"Yes, it is beyond the physical, Rainier, she is hurt to the bottom of her soul."

Prince Rainier and Father Tucker were speaking about the physical distress and near depression Princess Grace experienced after learning of the universal criticism of her decision to make another movie.

"What can we do to help her?"
   "We can only stand by and pray. Right now, we cannot

console her, talk with her, reason with her. It is her private agony, Rainier. It is Grace's Garden."

"Garden! Agony! Do you mean Gethsemane?"

"Yes! Precisely! Hers is a religious crisis. I hope to God she sees it that way. Gethsemane means allegorically a form of death followed by a newer, higher living."

"Please, Father, must we be so mystical? I want no talk of death. My wife is ill because of my poor decision and because I mishandled the press."

"Rai, I assure you that Grace's conflict, her agony, were inevitable, if not now, then later. You, me, the press, all of us, never know as we act freely at our own level that we may be the agents of Divine Providence on another. The mystical can be practical when it is the key to understanding."

"Profound, Father, profound! Please share with me your mystical insight. For God's sake, I want to help her."

"You have already helped her. You alone have stood by her, supported her, shown your love for her. You, alone, placed her first. That is her only consolation at this time of abandonment and grief. You could not have done more for her than that. I respect you for it. No more personal recriminations, Rai. She will call for you and you alone."

"I will be there, believe me, she means more to me than life. But I cannot just wait for her to call, I must do something. At least, I must understand and know what to expect. What is happening?"

"A beautiful, beautiful child is dying. The lovely little Grace of fancy, fairy tales, clever rhymes, lovely reveries, and of determination, grit, and artistic excellence. Yes, the little girl in Grace is dying. A sacrificial offering by the mature Grace for the good of us all. Few of us are called to make such a sacrifice. Only the death of the children or you could grieve her more."

"I catch your meaning, Father. If you are right, it is a spiritual conflict, a Gethsemane, a Divine calling. But let's consider practical consequences. What if she does not accept?"

"I doubt that she can make the picture now. The joy is gone. But if she yields only to external pressure, she will be outwardly accepting but inwardly very unhappy, possibly bitter. God knows she has a right to be. Her role as Princess would be an irksome burden, a reaction to losing her other role. Her consolation will be the children and you. She will have lost much of her zest for living, which is her charisma."

"And we were doing so well, doing so well! Why couldn't Hitchcock leave us alone?"

"Don't blame Al, Rainier. His is another unwitting role in our Divine Comedy. He means well by Grace and you. He and his set have no real understanding of what Grace and you have here and, I do not doubt, will never understand the sacrifice I think she will make."

"Ah, the Sacrifice! If she makes it, what then?"

"Then you will be married to a great woman, indeed! She will be ready to devote herself completely to family and principality with no other career draw. I suspect she may be less exuberant as she makes her compensations for the little girl that died, but she will find them. What will you do with such a woman?"

"Father, that's the woman I thought I had all along. She will be my partner more than ever. She is smarter than me in many ways. And you, too, if I may be so frank."

"Since you have been, you may be. Hear me well, now. Grace's offering and her self-sacrifice will mean that she has made her own private sacramental commitment to Princess just as the two of you together made a sacramental commitment to be partners in marriage. If she makes that commitment you will

have to make it too. Then you will be sacramental Prince and Princess as well as sacramental married partners. The two will merge as one sacramental commitment."

"That is a beautiful thought, Father. In my own way, I long for it. I can assure you I have no wish for anything else."

"Rai, the two of you will knock them dead. Once you are on your way, you can forget about allegories, Gardens, even the conscious awareness of sacrament. You will make it all happen! You can wrap the Council around you fingers, floor that game-playing Greek, and kick the Premier right in the ass. You will have a helluva good time. Grace will love it."

"I'm ready for her call now, Father. I'm ready; God, am I ready."

"Good! Good! Tell me, your Serene Highness, wouldn't you love to see someone goose Charles De Gaulle?"

Astonished were Grace Kelly's closest friends, her Manhattan buddies, to learn that she was to make another film. Having accompanied her to Monaco for her wedding, they were certain when pageant and ceremony ended that the "good old days" were over. They wept as they saw her stand regally by Prince Rainier at the opera in Monte Carlo at a gala following their civil wedding ceremony on April 8, 1956.

Gant Gaither wrote,

"Her Serene Highness, Princess of Monaco, wore a bugle beaded gown by Lanvin, a coronet of diamonds, and the fragile necklace that was a gift from the people of Monaco. With the Order of Saint Charles across her chest, Grace Kelly the movie star has vanished."

There was to be no Hollywood Tomorrow. Then that September she made it official.

It was not until she arrived again in Paris, the September after her marriage, en route to the United States, that the Princess of Monaco answered the question in everybody's mind. She declared that her career as a motion picture star was "definitely over." Until that moment no one had known for sure.

Her friends could only conclude that the combination of the role of "Marnie" and direction by Hitchcock overwhelmed her. They could testify that "her ability to know what role is 'right' for her has always been remarkable." (McCollum)

Though surprised at her decision, they would not be surprised at her reaction to the universal disapproval of it, for they knew how their friend Grace reacted to controversy better than anyone — better than family, husband, chaplain, or manager. They had been with her through lesser controversies before. A series of quotes from Gant Gaither's *Princess of Monaco*, published in 1957, reveals with uncanny accuracy how Princess Grace in 1962 would meet her greatest crisis.

Grace hates unpleasantness, and she absolutely cannot argue or fight; it makes her physically ill ...

When the world became too much for her, Grace had always turned to her church. Watching her regain her strength through its strength, no one could ever discredit the power of faith — whatever the inspiration. Once again she found new courage with which to face the inevitable problems of life ...

Grace has always cherished the peace that comes with receiving Communion at daybreak, no matter where she is — whether in South America, Hollywood, or New York ...

She was disappointed but instead of moping about it, she was off to the next project. For even at an ordinary game of cards, a little cloud crosses Grace's face momentarily when she's losing, and she fights to get back to a winning status. Many people spend so much time justifying their defeats that life passes them by before they can get back on the track. Nothing like that ever happened with Grace Kelly ...

Whatever the setbacks might have been, Grace quickly brushed them aside, without wasting any time wallowing in self pity ...

Of her struggle with the "Marnie" dilemma, Grace herself said, "I've often thought to myself that if I ever let go at times like that, I'd never come up again."

With her final decision to forgo "Marnie," Grace was close to letting go. She rose again — but left a little of Grace Kelly behind.

—16—
Breaking Away 1962 to 1964

There has been much speculation as to why Canon Tucker decided to leave the limelight in Europe to return to obscurity in the United States.

In his letters to "Dear Joe," he had often referred to his desire to come home for home's sake. By 1962, he was becoming free of many responsibilities in Monaco and Rome (including being chaplain of the Yacht Club of Monaco). His term as General Councillor for the Oblates had expired in August 1961. Having engineered a worthy successor to the old Superior General, he could distance himself from that office.

The death of Cardinal Tardini was a blow to Father Tucker in his career as a Vatican diplomat. Tardini, had he lived, is likely to have been the papal successor to Pope John XXIII rather than Cardinal Montini, Paul VI.

Pope John XXIII is alleged to have said to Father Tucker, "I have no hat that fits you," meaning "I have no Cardinal's hat for you." Tardini, as Pope, may have found such a slot. So Father Tucker saw no new role for himself in Rome.

Another reason for leaving was personally reported to Brother Joe. Charles de Gaulle had shown his displeasure at the "American pressure" around the Prince by not inviting Canon Tucker to a political, social affair to which he would have expected to be invited. He concluded that in his role as advisor and unofficial "Secretary of State" he could become more a burden than a help to the Prince. His diplomatic mission was ended. Prince Rainier did not agree with that assessment.

The job of chaplain to the Royal Family required a younger man. A Royal Chaplain is expected to accompany a Royal Family on its travels and vacations. Father Tucker had been able to do that only occasionally. And with the "Marnie" affair over, he had no concern about the stability of the marriage of Grace and Rainier.

He had a desire to help the American Province to which he was returning. The Province had acquired an old resort hotel in Wernersville, Pennsylvania to use as a Retreat House. Father Tucker had no equal as a Retreat Master for both clergy and laity. (He found that he had a real job at the Retreat House, but he was not the Director. For the first time in over 40 years, he was not a boss — a victim of his own "over age" strategy.)

He may have had concerns about his health, though we cannot be certain about that. In any case, he had his reasons.

His family did not agree. Brother Joe urged him to stay in Monaco and/or Rome. Possibly as an advisor to the Monaco legation in Rome. He need not continue as pastor of Saint Charles Church, but he could be Canon and Legate, if not chaplain. Joe knew that there would be no status role for him in the States. Joe was right about that, but the health problems that arose shortly after Father Tucker's homecoming probably would have assured his return to the USA.

Saint-Charles
Monte Carlo
May 1st, 1962

My dear LORD PRINCE:
With Bishop Barthe's letter of approval in hand, as submitted to Your Highness' attention, and with the permission of my Superiors, may I now humbly petition Your Highness to agree to my release from active duty at Saint Charles' parish to the pastorate of which Your Highness appointed me by sovereign ordinance twelve years ago.

This appointment was occasioned and made possible by the fact that the Oblate Institute in August 1949 had elected me a Councillor General with residence in Rome for the same period of time. An indult from the Holy See permitted me to fulfill both functions concurrently.

At the General Chapter of the Oblates held in Assisi last August, the electors agreed to my request not to be considered for re-election because of my age and other personal reasons. These same reasons, my Lord Prince, apply to my respectful request by these presents, all the more because the American Province of the Oblates to which I belong from its foundation as a charter-member since 1906 now reclaims me.

Bishop Barthe has asked that my release from active duty

not sever the ties that bind me to his Cathedral as one of its Canons.

Your Highness knows that nothing could ever weaken the "bond of dilection" that holds me close to Your person, to Your Family, and to Your people.

Gratefully and devotedly,
JFT

A request in writing. The Prince seems to have been the last in line of those from whom approval was required.

July 8, 1962

My dear beloved Lord Prince:
How I have longed to talk to You, write to You! If I haven't, it is because I have been anxiously waiting, day to day, word from Father Buckley about the entente he was to have with Your Highness and the Bishop concerning the Oblates' agreement with the Vatican, through our then Superiors General, Father Balducelli and Cardinal Tardini, to continue our services in the Principality for another ten years, that is until 1970.

This agreement, from the beginning of 1950, entrusted to the Superior General of the Oblates the naming of the personnel to Saint Charles subject, of course, to the approval of the Prince and the Bishop. The removal, however, of any religious from any assignment is reserved by Canon Law to the Superior General, excepting the case where the Holy See might intervene.

This explains, my dear Lord Prince, my departure as of June first. I was under Obedience to do so.

I had long since asked to be relieved of the pastorate of Saint Charles. Your Highness agreed to this. As far as I know to date, the question of my successor awaits approval.

I am sure, my dear Lord Prince, that Your Highness can count on Father Buckley's fullest cooperation in the matter of the Oblates' services at your command.

It was he who, as American Provincial, provided me through the 12 years with the help of men from his province, Fathers Shugrue, Bowler, La Penta, Boston, O'Connell, and others through vacations and times we needed substitutions, when the former Superior General was unable to draw help elsewhere. Now, as Superior General himself, Father Buckley will not fail You — least of all, in my regard.

Superiors General themselves are under obligation to the Sacred Congregation of Religious. Your Highness is acquainted with the policy of the Holy See touching on relations between the Episcopate and Religious Orders. This policy was delicately and charitably applied in the present case which so intimately interested the welfare of the Church in the Principality and out of it.

As Bishop Barthe declared, my departure cannot sever the ties that bind me to Monaco's Cathedral — and, may I add, much less those that bind me to Monaco's Prince!

With deep affection to all my "Other Family,"
JFT

Actually, there seems to have been some delay in arranging a final departure of Father Tucker from Monaco. He seems to have "commuted" several times between the United States, Rome, and Monaco through 1963.

"TUCKER TO RETURN TO MONACO"

The Very Reverend J. Francis Tucker will leave in about a week to return to his pastorate of Saint Charles Church, Monte Carlo.

But Father Tucker, who is 74, hopes to come back this year to spend the rest of his life working among old friends in his native Wilmington.

YESTERDAY, Father Tucker made arrangements with the Very Reverend John J. Conmy, superior of the American Province of the Oblates of Saint Francis de Sales, to get back to Monaco for the Jan. 27 Feast of Santa Devota, patron of the little Mediterranean principality.

Father Tucker completed his first 12-year assignment to Saint Charles Church last year and was reappointed for another 12 years. This is the only church in the world immediately under the jurisdiction of the Oblate Mother House in Rome, which assigns the pastor with the concurrence of the Vatican Secretary of State. Both must release him if Father Tucker is to come home.

HE IS ALSO Canon of the Cathedral of the Immaculate Conception in Monaco, an appointment made by the Bishop of Monte Carlo in agreement with Prince Rainier.

Priests never retire as long as they are physically able to perform an assignment. Father Conmy said "Father Tucker has tremendous vigor, we would love to have him here, and his experience as pastor, teacher and administrator would make him invaluable."

◆◆◆

Vatican
Oct. 15, 1963

Again "in the middle" of all this and all these — with one foot in heaven, and the other dragging through the earthly Eternal City. Love to all, well and happy.

JFT

213

"In the middle of all this" referred to sessions of the 2nd Vatican Council to which Canon Tucker served as an advisor. With Doctorates in both philosophy and theology, he was an expert on liturgical functions. He later told a relative that the changes in liturgy proposed by the Council were intended for missions in developing countries and not for locations that had established parishes and churches. He could foresee that the liturgical changes, widely implemented, would make obsolete many cathedrals and parish churches.

It is not feasible to do "theater in the round" in an old-style music hall.

◆◆◆

View From The Pew

Oh leave me alone with my Missal
I just want to kneel here and pray.
The others can sing when you whistle
But I like the old Catholic way.

They need such a man on the wireless
To follow a Colt forward pass
But brother it certainly riles us
To be told what is happening at Mass.

I thought that my participation
Could best be done with a Mass book
But now with this great agitation
Our Sundays take on a new look.

When the priest prays to God with contrition
We burst out with one hymn of joy
And if you think it's some real competition
You are not liturgical, boy!

From the Fore Mass in anticipation
To the Mass of the Faithful all through,
This so-called lay participation
Just takes all the goodness from you.

We're sitting and singing and praying
Sometimes like we never know which.
And often we feel we'll be saying
It's just like we're singing with Mitch.

The liturgy boys have their session
Right now in the year sixty-three.
But soon they will learn a good lesson
And change all this picture for me.

Some day when the show is all over
And people get tired of this fuss
The old school will really recover
And give back the true Mass to us.

But now while they sing and they whistle
I still like the old Catholic way.
Please leave me alone with my Missal
I just want to kneel here and pray.

Cathy Cumen

But his particular concern that the implementation of untested theological approaches would undermine the "sense of priesthood" for many priests was prophetic. Nuns, too, were forced to discover personally that "sense of mission."

In 1968, Father Tucker said to nephew Joe, "The Church is in trouble." A sad statement from one whose main LOVE it was.

215

Monte-Carlo
Nov 6, 63

Dear Joe,
Your letter of Oct. 19 was forwarded from Hotel Minerva,
which I left on 26th, to the Palace at Monaco and was in hand
today.
    Masses for Tom Leonard said. Have had a very satisfying
trip all through. Am very grateful and happy over it. But I
want to go home! Bad weather, cold, damp, and so I'm leaving
Nov. 20, to arrive Pan American 155 at Philadelphia the 21st.
News later.
    Love to all
    JFT

To our knowledge, this was his final trip to Monaco. He returned to take up his assignment in Wernersville full-time.

Father Tucker, too, was deeply hurt by the assassination of President John Kennedy in November, 1963. He wrote this beautiful poem.

♦♦♦

A Letter From Heaven
Special Delivery From Heaven

    TO: THE KENNEDY FAMILY
    FROM: JOHN FITZGERALD KENNEDY

    Sorry I had to leave right away,
    I look down and smile at you every day.
    Little Patrick says to say "HI."
    I love you, I'm happy,
    So please don't cry.

And Caroline I'd like to say,
How proud Daddy was of you that day.
When you stood like a lady
And watched me go by,
And doing as Mommy, you tried not to cry.

Little John, now you're the big man,
Take care of Mommy the best you can.
You were just like a soldier
That salute was so brave.
Thanks for the flag that you put on my grave.

And Jackie, I had not time for good-by,
But I'm sure you could read the
'Farewell' in my eyes.
Watch over our children and love them for me,
I'll treasure your love through eternity.

So please carry on as you did before,
Till all of us meet on Heaven's bright shore.
Remember I love you, remember I care,
I'll always be with you,
Though you don't see me there.

◆◆◆

Wernersville, Pennsylvania
July 1st, 1964

To His Serene Highness RAINIER III
Prince Sovereign of Monaco.

My Lord Prince:

In date of February 15th this year, Your Highness graciously acknowledged my request of the beginning of the year that I be permitted to submit my resignation as Ecclesiastical Councillor of the Legation of the Prince of Monaco to the Holy See. Your Highness showed an affectionate reluctance to the consideration of this request and suggested a delay over it.

A month ago, I suffered a slight stroke, the doctors claimed from a bit of over-exertion in the discharge of my work as Retreat-Master for priests and laymen entailing extensive displacements across the USA. The Doctors insist on curtailing my travel and lessening my schedule of work.

In view of this "Act of God," may I not again pressure to ask Your Highness to acquaint the Holy See with my request, offered with profound gratitude and lasting appreciation to the exalted Parties devoutly served by our Legation.

That resignation ended completely his mission to Monaco. In the late Spring of 1966, he did make a trip to Rome, his final visit there. Niece Betty recalls that he visited her family in Paris on his way home. The same lively, ornery Uncle Francis. We do not know if he visited Monaco on this trip. He is unlikely to have done so if the Prince and Princess were not there.

Betty reports that he spent two days in Paris. Betty and friends chauffeured him about. He joined Bill for lunch at S.H.A.P.E. headquarters with a group of Allied officers. They were impressed that he could speak to each of them in his own language.

This chapter concludes with a handwritten letter from Princess Grace.

August 2nd 1966

Dear Father -

It was so nice to hear from you and I was glad to hear that the visit of the Cardinal Daugherty High School looked well on TV. I have had reports that they were not too pleased with their reception here. I do not think that the mayor handled it too well — I am very sorry that some were displeased. They are a very talented group, and terribly sweet and young. Those wonderful Irish American good looks!!

This Century year has been a great strain on strength, endurance and nerves. I am beginning to give away at the seams and have decided that ten days at Ocean City will put the roses back in my cheeks. We hope to get there in September.

Stephanie is a dream babe, but very active and on the move every minute. I had two of my brother's children and young Charles all here for three weeks and now suddenly the place seems so quiet without them.

Our children are in Ireland for their summer camp and seem to be enjoying it very much — even the rain.

Our American week went well. Ambassador Bohlen was here from Paris and the Dukes from Madrid. They all played baseball and am sure they were as stiff as I was the three days that followed.

The weather has not been very good this summer — although better than anywhere else. We are just spoiled.

Please remember me to Joe and Edna. We think of you often with much affection.

Grace

—17—
The Final Years 1964 to 1972

Canon Tucker celebrated his 75th birthday on January 8, 1964. He was in residence at the Villa Maria Oblate Retreat House in Wernersville, Pennsylvania. Villa Maria was purchased by the Wilmington Province of the Oblates to be a laymen's Retreat House. The Reverend John J. Green was its first director. Obviously, Father Conmy, the Oblate Provincial, would want the services of a premier Retreat Master like Canon Tucker to help put Villa Maria "on the map." The Canon took to his new assignment with characteristic vigor, but illness, that first and subsequent mini strokes, weakened him.

On a sleeting, icy January day in 1964, Joe and Edna celebrated their 50th wedding anniversary with Mass and a reception at the Salesianum High School. Later, Father Francis celebrated with them.

Having been controversial in Monaco for 13 years, he could now be controversial at home. In 1964, the Wilmington Morning News had this headline, "Priest hits violence in racial protests." The article by William P. Frank follows:

A Wilmington Catholic priest who has never been known to shy away from controversy lashed out last night at uncontrolled racial demonstrations. As the principal speaker at the Saint Patrick's Day dinner of the Friends of Ireland, the Very Reverend J. Francis Tucker said: "Last night's television news showed jungle-like scenes of school children of New York and Brooklyn engaged in boycotting the schools and marching on the building of the Board of Education.

"THIS TYPE of conduct and others denote a flagrant, corrupt, immoral, uncivilized and surely un-American concept of liberty."

The Gold Ballroom of the Hotel Du Pont was packed with men and women of all faiths to honor Saint Patrick. Among the guests were the Catholic and Episcopal bishops of this area — Bishop Michael W. Hyle of the Wilmington Catholic Diocese, and Bishop J. Brooke Mosley of the Episcopal Diocese of Delaware.

Father Tucker is now director of the Oblate retreat house at Wernersville, Pennsylvania.

IN HIS USUAL style, Father Tucker opened his talk with considerable humor and self-kidding. He described himself as a sort of prodigal son. "I've been farmed out again," he said, "by my Oblate superiors to the Retreat House in Wernersville, and all this because in their zeal for the salvation of my soul, their better judgment led them to decide that after 12 years of dissipation in Monte Carlo, I needed a retreat for the rest of my days."

Father Tucker had been in Monaco for a dozen years as the chaplain of Prince Rainier and Princess Grace, from whom he received Saint Patrick's Day greetings yesterday.

BUT AFTER his humorous introduction, Father Tucker took up the issue of boycott demonstrations and how the Irish had met discrimination and prejudice.

"What races," he asked, "have had more fun poked at them, more jokes invented at their expense, more comedy enacted in mimicry than the Irish?

"We emulated the wisdom of Solomon and laughed with those who laughed at us and kept on marching in The Mummers Parade." This last remark drew applause. Father Tucker continued:

"I ADD TO this that the melting pot was never meant to have the qualities of a goulash whose component parts are cut, ground, chopped and crushed into a pulp.

"The melting pot was rather intended to have the quality of an Irish stew whose ingredients retain their native individuality, and their identity — a potato remains a potato; an onion remains an onion; a turnip, a turnip; and to be sure, you don't mix in any sour grapes or poison."

221

Continuing along the same line, Father Tucker said, "We Irish, too, have suffered from educational inequality in more ways than one. And how did we meet that? Our parochial schools are the answer. We chose to respect others by our own self-respect."

The theme of Father Tucker's talk was, "There is good in forgiveness and evil in hatred." Father Tucker's remarks sparked this letter to the news:

At the Saint Patrick's Day dinner of the Friends of Ireland, Father Tucker drew the analogy between other minority groups and today's Negro.

No one will deny that all minority groups have endured discrimination. However, no group can lay claim to having endured discrimination at such length or in such large doses as the Negro. Perhaps if they were required to wear a shamrock or the star of David planted square in the middle of their foreheads, the same discrimination would be in evidence, but the fortuitous lack of any easily identifiable outward mark spares them.

I must take issue with Father Tucker's statement, "We emulated the wisdom of Solomon and laughed with those who laughed at us and kept marching in the Mummer's Parade." Come, come, Father — How long would you have marched if, in order to qualify, you had to wear a big red nose or carry a wash tub under your arm while you played "When Irish Eyes Are Smiling?"

I think Father Tucker will agree that it's much easier to deal with inequality while you're dining in the Gold Ballroom than when you're traveling through at dinner time looking for a place to eat and hoping you'll find a restaurant willing to accommodate you.

BLANCHE STOKES
Monroe Park

Ms. Stokes made her point brilliantly. But, some 35 years later, there are movements in the Afro-American Communities that suggest that Father Tucker was right in his social philosophy.

✦✦✦

Father Tucker had spartan but comfortable living quarters at the Wernersville Retreat House. His awards and medals were on prominent display. And the Oblates and their properties continued to grow. The new Salesianum prospered. A new wing was added to Northeast Catholic High School in Philadelphia. Father Tucker preached at its dedication with Archbishop John F. Krol presiding.

Saint Anthony of Padua parish, Wilmington, Delaware celebrated its "First Forty Years" at Christmas 1964. The major event was a solemn Midnight Anniversary Mass with Father Tucker, founder and first pastor, as celebrant. Saint Anthony's now had a complete church, a rectory, elementary school, a girls high school, Padua Academy, and a large social hall. The Italians had done it all. There was, of course, an Anniversary Banquet.

If anything, Uncle Francis' concern for family grew stronger on his return to the United States. He had a particular concern for the grandnephews and grandnieces of his brother Ed. With both parents gone, he was concerned about their welfare and that of their children. In November 1965, he wrote a grandnephew recommending action to be taken to keep his father's family together. In that letter he wrote: "I'm a sick man or I would be closer to all of you." Even so, he continued working and in 1966 visited Rome and Paris once more. And found time to send Valentine cards to his grandnieces.

✦✦✦

By 1969, Father Francis' health had deteriorated to the extent that he needed assistance with aspects of personal care. He moved to the faculty house at Salesianum Catholic High School, Wilmington, Delaware, where such care could be provided to him and several other aging Oblates.

He had a small, comfortable single room. He was cared for by Oblate brothers, men of compassion and thick skin. He continued to be both newsworthy and event worthy.

In June 1969, The University of Delaware at its Commencement Exercises conferred an Honorary Doctor of Laws degree on John Francis Tucker, the second such award he had received. The first, many years earlier, was conferred by Mount Saint Mary's College, Maryland.

In 1969, on his 80th birthday, he had a short interview with Tom Malone, a reporter for the Wilmington Morning News.

"Thrasher Out 'Pill,' Says Father Tucker" by Tom Malone

Debate over birth control and marriage of the clergy in the Catholic Church is a necessity in the mind of the Reverend Dr. J. Francis Tucker.

"We have to have it out and get it over with," he said yesterday on a quiet day at Salesianum School, where he was marking his 80th birthday.

Father Tucker is one of Delaware's best known clergymen, generally credited as one of the leaders in the nationwide buildup of the Oblates of Saint Francis de Sales — the order of priests which teaches at Salesianum.

Slowed down a bit by flu (the Honolulu flu, he called it: "What I have is much closer to home than Hong Kong"), the wit he has shown in his 58 years as a priest still breezes through his conversation.

The controversy within the Catholic Church brought no show of excitement from him. "It's another generation, another sign of the changes in a new generation," he said. "The constants remain."

Thrashing out the problems "might take 10 years, but it has to be done. Sixty years ago when I was 20, you had to prove yourself innocent. Today you have to be proved guilty. I think that's an advance."

He did take exception to those who argue that one should follow his conscience. "There is such a thing as an erroneous conscience." He likes everything he has seen about ecumenism. "I think I had some ecumenical experience of my own in my time. I was speaking in churches of all denominations years ago."

There could be a natural follow-up to it, in his mind.

"As you head down the Peninsula you see all these small towns dotted with three, four churches, all of different denominations. All this property for churches. I think churches could share their buildings. They do it in Switzerland. They do it in the military service. I think it's something that could be examined."

As he talked — making it clear that these were random thoughts — he touched on the generation gap.

He has spent many of his years among boys of high school age and as far as he's concerned, "I believe sincerely in the innate decency of our boys and girls today.

"But one thing I have stressed in every talk to boys' schools, girls' schools. That is: 'Don't create sin'."

To Father Tucker, sin is something that defies what to him is the natural law, goes against the Commandments, tears at the fabric of the sacraments of his church.

"But us older ones, we set up arbitrary standards of good and evil, standards that have grown up around us without our realizing it. We've tried to impose them on the younger ones and some of them, they just aren't having.

"They say there's greater frankness today. I can't give a definite answer on that. Perhaps there is, but perhaps, within limits, it's good.

"But we spend so much time on arguing about the immaterial, the short skirts of the girls, the long hair of the boys."

Here he put in a footnote. Passing a hand over the gloss on his scalp, he said, "They say wigs are coming back. Now there's no reason for me to be against that."

He is living at Salesianum now, greeting priests he once knew as students, greeting students to inquire for their grandfathers.

✦✦✦

Obviously, his mind was clear and active, though he did have occasional episodes of disorientation and forgetfulness which caused him to be anxious and defensive.

Privately, he was very concerned about the turmoil in the church. "My church is in trouble," he remarked to this writer at that time. In a sense the church had become "unglued." He was particularly concerned about the departure of massive numbers of priests and nuns from the vocational callings. His own Oblates of Saint Francis de Sales was having many departures from its ranks.

Tom Malone wrote another article based on his interview with Father Tucker titled "Does TV hurt retreats?" Though a little repetitive of the previous article, it too has its moments.

Father Tucker, 80, Reminisces

"Two of the main ingredients of a good religious education are a sound teacher and a good cook,"Father Tucker said yesterday.

"I shouldn't be giving any opinions, really," he said. "I've spent the night with an ice pack, one on my shoulder where the doctor stabbed me. Most of the time I was thinking uncharitable things about doctors."

This was the Very Reverend Dr. J. Francis Tucker at home, celebrating his 80th birthday.

Home is the Salesianum School, where Father Tucker agreed to talk about his 58 years in the Catholic priesthood, and about Prince Rainier and Princess Grace of Monaco, and the possible interference with Catholic religious retreats by televised football games of Notre Dame and other teams.

While he was talking, four feminine members of the staff — Mrs. Concetta Chromey, librarian; Mrs. James McGuinness, assistant librarian, Mrs. Alice B. Reese, secretary — filed in, bearing gifts and singing, "Happy Birthday ..."

His smile kept widening as he let them sing it through. He thanked them and asked how they liked his robe. It was a blue robe with white splashes, worn over a red checked sport shirt, black clerical trousers and glossy black loafers.

They left after he had warned them against doctors, and hinted at refreshments later in the day.

At 80, Father Tucker can be regarded as one of the senior statesmen among Delaware clergy. He is the best known Catholic priest in the Wilmington diocese, and in a state possessive of being first, he has a list of firsts of his own:

— The first student at Salesianum School, which he entered in 1903. "I was going to go to Saint Joe Prep in Philly, but the late Father Lyons at Saint Peter's told me, 'Try the Frenchies,' and I've never been sorry."

– The first American to be ordained a priest of the Oblates of Saint Francis de Sales, an order that now counts more than 1,000 American priests in two North American provinces with missionaries in South America and Africa.

– The founder of Saint Anthony's Catholic Church.

– The first American provincial of the Oblates in North America.

– The first American to be named chaplain to the court of Monaco.

"The Monagasques are Italian in background — the Grimaldi family — and I must say I never got along too well with the French. My feeling for them was returned. One morning I woke up and found a sign, 'Yankee, go home,' scrawled on the rectory."

He still hears from the prince and princess.

"I had a fruit cake from them just before Christmas. It was delicious. I looked at the label. It was Neiman-Marcus of Dallas. Ah, those Texans."

There are those who claim persuasively that Father Tucker is primarily responsible for the growth of his order in the United States but Father Tucker — "and anyone can tell you I've never been one for false humility" — won't have it.

"We've been blessed here by our antecedents," he said, referring to Fathers Isenring, Fromentin and Jacquier, the three French priests who formed Salesianum here.

And he said, "I'd call Tommy Lawless the artisan of our growth," a reference to the late Very Reverend Dr. Thomas A. Lawless, who became an Oblate a year after Father Tucker.

In the conversation, Father Tucker became serious at times, but only in answering serious questions. He believes in absolute values in life, but doubts that long hair for boys and short skirts for girls are burning issues.

This was a festive time, so he guided the conversation back to the light line with his light touch, as when he was talking about recent falling off in attendance at spiritual retreats among Catholic laymen.

That was when he brought in his reference to some ingredients for religious instruction. "A good retreat house needs a good cook," he said. "You have to nourish the mind, but you have to feed the animal."

Any drop in attendance could, to his mind, be nothing more than timing.

"They hold retreats from Friday nights to Sunday nights," he said. "Do you realize what that means to so many men and boys? It means missing the college games Saturday and the pros on TV Sunday. That could be the reason, no more than that."

✦✦✦

At age 80 in 1970, Father Tucker celebrated the 59th anniversary of his ordination to the priesthood. The most significant event was a concelebrated Mass with fellow Oblates at the Salesianum School in which he resided. The following was his response to felicitations from Joe and Edna.

Your greetings and good wishes for my anniversary were deeply appreciated. Wishing you every blessing,
  Sincerely,
  Father J. Francis

✦✦✦

This is the family's only record of his "J. Francis" signature.

Nineteen seventy-one was a Jubilee Year for Father Tucker, marking the 60th Anniversary of his ordination to the priesthood, a span that very few priests have achieved. Though the actual anniversary date was August 10, 1971, his Oblate confreres chose Sunday, May 2nd, 1971 to be the time for a concelebrated Mass of Thanksgiving to be held at Saint Anthony of Padua Church followed by a Testimonial Dinner at Fournier Memorial Hall. Both were by invitation only. The Testimonial Mass at four o'clock had the Bishop of Wilmington, The Most Reverend Thomas J. Mondaga, DD, as Principal Celebrant. Father Tucker was a concelebrant along with all key Oblate leaders, the Superior General, Assistant Superior General, Provincial, Counselors, and a host of local clergy. The Offertory Procession was led by Mr. and Mrs. Joseph Tucker, Sr., and family.

This Mass was a tribute by the Oblates of Saint Francis de Sales to a "founding father" whose life reflected in extraordinary ways the "spiritual rule" they lived by.

It was as proclaimed, a Mass of Thanksgiving. Webster's second meaning of the word testimonial — something given or done as an expression of esteem, admiration or gratitude — certainly applied to the Testimonial Dinner honoring "The Very Reverend Canon J. Francis Tucker, OSFS, on the 60th anniversary of his Holy Ordination to the Priesthood" that followed the Anniversary Mass.

  Refreshments 5:00 p.m. — Tuckian Room
  Dinner 6:00 p.m. — Fournier Memorial Hall

Several hundred guests attended the dinner. There were 32 "Jubilee Celebration Guests." These included the Bishop of Wilmington and key Oblate and secular clergy, the State of Delaware Congressional Delegation (both Senators and Representatives), the Governor, the New Castle County Executive, Mayor of Wilmington, and President of the City Council.

At the head table were Mr. and Mrs. Joseph Tucker, Sr., representing the Canon's family, and Mrs. John B. Kelly, Sr., representing "that other family" in Monaco. Of particular satisfaction to the Canon was the presence of three old religious protagonists and friends. The Very Reverend Arthur McKinstry, DD, Retired Episcopal Bishop of Wilmington, the Reverend Dr. Park Huntington, DD, Ph.D, Pastor Emeritus, Saint Stephens Lutheran Church, and Mrs. Huntington and Rabbi and Mrs. Hebert Drooz, Congregation Beth Emeth.

Table 25 was reserved for the many nieces, nephews, grandnieces, and grandnephews of Canon Tucker who were able to attend. Many had never previously met.

The dinner program included three speakers and a response by Canon Tucker. Though obviously quite feeble, he walked in small steps to the podium and one final time displayed his wit and humor in a tribute to those who were honoring him. Following the dinner, he had a convivial private meeting with Rabbi Drooz, Reverend Mr. McKinstry, and Reverend Huntington. It is reported that Mrs. Kelly was shocked by the physical weakness of Father Tucker and reported so to Princess Grace.

This was the last major public appearance of Uncle Francis to his family's knowledge. In January 1972, he attended the wedding of his grandniece, Judy Tucker, a granddaughter of Joe and Edna, at Saint Anthony's Church, by his presence in the Sanctuary during the Wedding Mass.

❖❖❖

Brother Joe and other family members would visit Father Francis at Wernersville as often as they could. Joe's sons, Cliff and Joe, Jr., on occasion would drive their father to Wernersville. On one visit, Joe tried to persuade his Uncle Francis to write his memoirs or dictate them. We are certain that he did not do so. In 1967, the mini strokes became more frequent, requiring Father Francis to have physical care by Oblate brothers. At Christmas, 1967, Joe, Edna and the families of sons Joe and Cliff went to Wernersville to spend the Holidays with him. This permitted the Oblate residents to make home visits for Christmas. It was Tucker only for a few days. Mary and Phyllis took over in the ancient institutional kitchen. Uncle Francis was well enough to celebrate Christmas Mass with the grandnephews Kevin and Gregory serving as altar boys and John making the spiritual readings. Christmas dinner included turkey and trimmings. A few unforgettable days. Sister Betty and family were in Europe, to everyone's regret.

When Father Tucker's health deteriorated to the point that he could no longer participate in Retreats, his Oblate confreres persuaded him to become a resident in the faculty house of the Salesianum School, Wilmington, Delaware. There medical care was more available and personal care more easy to provide. Brother Mike and other saintly souls were the caregivers. As his health declined, he became more of a Hickey (irascible, verbally abusive).

Even that was humorous. On one occasion, his grandnephews Bob, Dick, Kevin, and Greg were sent to visit him. Not knowing who these young giants were, he shouted "What a dirty trick to pull on an old man" and evicted them post haste. A chastening experience. He would be brought by car to visit Joe and Edna who lived just a few blocks away. Nephew Cliff was the long-suffering chauffeur for several of these visits. He reported that his beloved uncle would yell "don't touch me" and in general "give me hell" during that exercise.

During one stay at the Saint Anthony's hospital in Wilmington, Delaware, he was cared for by a loving Franciscan nun. One day she said to him, "I'm the best friend you have." He replied, "Madam, you most certainly are not." The last few months of his life were spent at the Tilton Terrace Nursing Home.

This writer met a young nun at a University summer session who said, "I took care of Father Tucker in his final illness." I replied, "That must have been colorful." She answered: "Oh! It wasn't too bad; I had an Irish Father."

Father Tucker died November 2, 1972 at the nursing home as he approached his 84th birthday. A family member, his nephew Cliff, was with him at the moment. He had been a priest for over 61 years.

His and our family friend, Monsignor Paul J. Taggart, wrote this guest editorial in the Delmarva Dialog dated November 10, 1972:

Farewell Friend

Merely to mention the name of the man is to bring a smile to the face of the hearers. That is, if they had ever known Father Tucker.

This is not to say he was a buffoon. By no means. But he had a wit, charm, a warmth, a humor, that implanted itself in the memory. He had a flare, a flamboyance, a sense of the dramatic, a sparkle that few could emulate but all would envy.

He would have loved his funeral — the governor, the major senators, civic leaders, incumbents and hopefuls — clergy of other faiths — cables and telegrams from across the nation and around the world, even from royalty whom he had married — literally thousands stopping by to visit with him for the last time, to pray within the arena of his greatest triumph. Not the church of Saint Anthony, but the real arena — his parish arena — his people of Wilmington.

Of course, he might have planned some aspects differently — might have timed things differently: the procession didn't wind all through "little Italy," there were no marching bands, no statues aloft on shoulder-carriers — there wasn't even a newspaper over that weekend to give the event full play!

Father Tucker was a man of many "firsts." The first student at Wilmington's famous Salesianum — the first American seminarian for the Oblates foundation in this country — the first pastor of Saint Anthony's parish — the first to locally found a CYO parish unit — the first to start a Wilmington Newman Club.

But these events are dated. In mind and heart he was also first in other areas now considered part of a clergyman's — a citizen's — way of life.

Before ecumenism had become a household word, he had crossed denominational lines, mounted other pulpits, counted as friends and companions-in-action leaders of local faiths, Christian and Jewish. An Episcopalian bishop, a Lutheran chaplain, a Methodist pastor, a rabbi subtly indicated a willingness to be among the speakers at any of his jubilees, and he was always having a jubilee of some sort these recent years!

If crime on the streets seems an issue of only recent moments, our memories are short. When Father Tucker was surveying the city for a site for his new church, people were also afraid to walk some streets at night. A Wilmington mayor, within memory, quoted figures of our Department of Safety to show that the advent of Father Tucker's work in the Saint Anthony area marked the almost-immediate turnabout in crime statistics. His follow-up of those who did tangle with the law made him a familiar figure in the courts and jails. He placed his reputation on the line for those he felt could be helped.

Unable for some years to provide Catholic schooling for his parish youngsters, he made his presence felt in the area of public education. He was unofficial chaplain for Wilmington High School and boasted of an honorary diploma presented by its students.

Before the day when civil rights and public morality claimed headlines, he took on the KKK, the Prohibitionists, various state professional associations, pornography in the theater and press. He never looked for a fight, but he never backed away from one, as the News Journal wrote editorially some years ago — and then cited issues on which he and they took opposite stands, vehemently, in public. But a relationship of mutual respect kept them working together for the good of the community.

Before public welfare had become an issue for debate, he resolved the problems of many by personal intervention, solicitation of funds from the well-to-do, family support, private charity. He lent the weight of his influence to the emerging state programs to make life more bearable for the poor, many of whom he had come to know personally in their distress.

In his sixty years as a priest, he roamed the highways of the world — many in person, others through his fellow Oblates whom he sent out to new mission fields as the Province, under his leadership, mushroomed.

He was first and foremost a priest interested in the people of God. What talents he had been entrusted with — wit and intellect, zest and personality, he returned to his Maker a hundred-fold in the service of others.

Monsignor Paul J. Taggart
Vicar General
Diocese of Wilmington

Bibliography

Primary source materials incorporated completely or in large part in the Text.

a. Over 80 personal letters and cards written to close relatives and others by Canon Tucker during his 12 years at Monaco.

b. Memoranda and letters between Prince Rainier and Canon Tucker

c. Log Book — Trip to Monaco, Joseph A. Tucker, 1958

d Letter — Princess Grace to Canon Tucker, 1966

e. Pre-publication article, "My Boy, the Prince of Monaco" by Canon Tucker, 1953

f. Article "Farewell, Friend," a tribute to Canon Tucker by Monsignor Paul J. Taggert, Delmarva Dialog, November 10, 1972

g. Gossip Column article by Dorothy Kilgallen, April1966

h. Reply to Ms. Kilgallen by Reverend Lawrence McCarthy, OSFS, 1956

I. Letters by Edna Tucker

j. Announcements from Oblates of Saint Francis de Sales

k. Appointments as chaplain of the Military Vicariate

References from which quotations, statements of historic events are included in the text.

a. Hawkins, Peter. *Prince Rainier of Monaco*. London: William Kimber, 1966.

b. Robyns, Gwen. *Princess Grace*. New York: David McKay Company, Inc., 1976.

c. Kelley, Kitty. *Elizabeth Taylor, The Last Star.* New York: Dell, 1981.

d. Gaither, Gant. *Princess Grace*. Hoft, 1956.

e. Robinson, Jeffrey. *Rainier and Grace, An Intimate Portrait.* New York, NY: A Morgan Entrekin Book, The Atlantic Monthly Press, 1989.

f. Sevindel, Larry. *The Last Hero, A Biography of Gary Cooper*. Garden City, New York: Double Day & Company, 1980.

g. McCollum, John. *That Kelly Family*. New York: A.S. Barnes & Co., 1957.

h. Burton, Katherine. *So Much So Soon*. New York: Benziger Brothers, 1953.

I. Zolotow, Maurice. "Grace Kelly's Biggest Gamble." *TheAmerican Weekly*, April 15, 1956.

j. *New Catholic Encyclopedia*, Washington, DC: CatholicUniversity of America, 1967.

k. *Grace Kelly*, Current Biography, 1955.

l. De Quenetain, Tanneguy. "How Far Is Cardinal Montini From The Papal Throne?" *Realities*, Number 138, 1962.

m. Groves, Charles. "Royal Riviera" Hfinemann Ltd, 1957.

n. Fielding, Temple. Fielding's Europe. New York: Fielding Publications, 1981.

o. Catholic Almanac, 1982.

References that can aid in comprehending the text.

Books

A. Englund, Steven. *Grace of Monaco*. Garden City, New York, NY: Double Day, 1984.

B. Hall, Trevor. *Her Serene Highness Princess Grace of Monaco*. London, England: Greenwich House, Key Stone Press, 1982.

C. Davis, Phyllida. Grace, *The Story of A Princess*. New York: St. Martin's Press, 1982.

E. Tornsbene, Lyn. *Long Live The King*. New York: Putnam's, 1976.

F. Shepard, Donald and Slatier, Robert. *Bing Crosby, The Hollow Man*. Pinuvele Books, 1981.

G. Lewis, Arthur. *Those Philadelphia Kelly's: With A Touch of Grace*. New York: William Morris, 1977.

H. Hoffecker, Carol *Wilmington. A Pictorial History*. Norfolk, VA: The Donning Co., 1982.

I. Fielding, Temple. French Riviera, Cote D'Azur. London: Michelen Tyre, 1974.

J. Jackson, Stanley. Inside Monte Carlo. New York: Stein and Day, 1976.

K. Fielding, Ian. The Money Spinner. Boston: Little Brown & Co., 1977.

L. Brogan, P.W. France: Life World Library. New York: Time Inc., 1960.

N. Life of His Holiness, Pope Pius X. New York: Benziger Brothers, 1904.

References, periodicals, newspapers, films, etc. containing articles about Princess Grace, Prince Rainier, Canon Tucker.

McCall's Magazine — 1954
Sign Magazine
Catholic Digest
Saturday Evening Post
Collier
Life
Parade
Paris Match
People Magazine
Philadelphia Inquirer
Philadelphia Bulletin
Wilmington Morning News
Wilmington Evening Journal
CBS Film, *A Look At Monaco,* 1963

Photographs
Tucker Family Archives and Hulton Getty Collection

Saint Anthony De Padua Church, Wilmington, Delaware

About the Author

Wandering after World War II, Joe Tucker met Mary Callnan by chance while she was on vacation in Colorado Springs in May 1946. Recognizing an answer to a prayer when he saw one, he followed her to Manhattan, where she lived and worked. They were wed in August 1947. Mary supported Joe while, using the GI Bill, he earned an M.A. from Teachers College and a Ph.D. in Educational Psychology from Columbia University. Joe subsequently worked in Military Human Factors, Systems Psychology with the Space Technology Laboratories, and Educational Technology in a number of industrial/business settings. As a late career endeavor, he directed the Center for Educational Technology, School of Education, Catholic University of America, and was a consultant for the Bio-medical and Behavioral Sciences Division of the Federal Aviation Administration.

Now mostly retired, Mary and Joe enjoy frequent contacts with their four children and five grandchildren.

Joseph A. Tucker, Jr. was born May 28, 1916, in Wilmington, Delaware and, in so doing, kept his father, Joe, Sr., from the World War I draft. His education was Catholic — grammar school, Sacred Heart; high school, Salesianum; college, Catholic University of America from which he earned a B.A. in Philosophy in 1939. He spent over six years as a seminarian with the Oblates of St. Francis de Sales. He enlisted in the Army Air Corps in 1942 and became an Aerial Navigation Instructor during most of the War. He left the service in December 1945 as a First Lieutenant.

Then he wandered until he met Mary, but he never forgot his uncle Francis and the Oblates of St. Francis de Sales. Hopefully, these two volumes will persuade his beloved uncle not to "kick his butt" all over Paradise.

Joseph A. Tucker, Jr.